Quick
Find
NIWC

PROJECT QUICK FIND

Memoirs
OF A U.S. NAVY SEAL
TRAINING SEA LIONS

MICHAEL P. WOOD

THE History PRESS

Published by The History Press
Charleston, SC
www.arcadiapublishing.com

Front cover: Author's photograph for *Skin Diver* magazine, showing a sea lion diving and implanting a D5 grabber onto the training ASROC target.

The majority of the photographs used in this book were taken by the author or are from the author's collection. There are some photographs from the collections of Rick Hetzell and Dan Peterson, as well as official U.S. Navy photos.

Manufactured in the United States

ISBN 9780738503547
Library of Congress Control Number: 2016948306

Notice: These are memoirs of a U.S. Navy SEAL training sea lions, and, as such, are based on the author's experiences with Project Quick Find. This is not a comprehensive history of Project Quick Find. The information in this book is true and complete to the best of our knowledge. It is offered without guarantee on the part of the author or Arcadia Publishing. The author and Arcadia Publishing disclaim all liability in connection with the use of this book.

In Memory of Chief Gordon Sybrant

DEDICATION

I would like to dedicate this book to all my fellow SEAL, EOD, and NUC marine mammal trainers and veterinarians, and our sea lion partners that made Project Quick Find possible. The NUC visionary development of the program, combined with the steadfast and hardworking military and civilian trainers and animals, made Project Quick Find a quick and long-lasting success story within the U.S. Navy for the recovery of objects on the sea floor. There are many civilian and military names that were instrumental, but the one that stands out the most during my time period in Quick Find was that of Chief Gordon Sybrant. Those of us Quick Find plank owners—John Busch, Tom McHugh, Rick Hetzell, Dan Peterson, and I—were all part of the Gordy Team that took Project Quick Find from beginning to final recognition and certification within the U.S. Navy.

CONTENTS

1
HISTORY

Naval Undersea Research and Development Center (NUC) Hawaii Laboratory initiated Project Quick Find, which was considered a marine mammal system for object recovery. The first shipment of sea lions for the program was delivered in September 1969, and the program development took from September 1969 until December 1970, when NUC conducted extensive sea lion behavioral conditioning in order to prepare the sea lions for all the projected tasks they would need to recover a designated object.

The NUC trainers needed to adapt the sea lions to captivity and use operant conditioning to teach twenty total tasks, including hand tame, harness, muzzle, recall strobe, cage conditioning, target hit, hear-tell 37 kHz, D3 target mark, open-water release, D4 target mark, center hit, D5 target mark, hear-tell 9 kHz, end hit, recall buzzers, depth to 250 feet, recovery exercises, depth 250–350 feet, depth 350–450 feet, and depth 450–500 feet.

In June 1972, the official NUC report on Project Quick Find was released, titled "A Marine Mammal System for Object Recovery." Martin E. Conboy from Ocean Sciences Department submitted the report, which stated: "Project Quick Find is a recovery system that consists of two men, a rubber boat, a reel of nylon line, a pinger receiver, a grabber device, and a California sea lion. It was developed to provide the Navy with an effective alternative to the use of divers and submersibles for the underwater recovery of small objects."

AD744232

NUC TP 268
Rev. 1

PROJECT QUICK FIND: A MARINE MAMMAL SYSTEM FOR OBJECT RECOVERY

by

Martin E. Conboy
Ocean Sciences Department
June 1972

Approved for public release; distribution unlimited.

Reproduced by
NATIONAL TECHNICAL INFORMATION SERVICE

Above: John Busch and Bill Rosecrans walk their sea lions at the facility in Hawaii.

Left: Official NUC report on Project Quick Find.

Table 1. Sea lions acquired by NUC.

No.	Name	Sex	Approximate Age, years	Weight, lb	Disposition
1	Akahi	male	2	67	Quick Find
2	Fatman	male	2	88	Quick Find
3	Sam	male	2	68	Quick Find (Lost animal)
4	Juneau	male	4	88	Quick Find (Died Dec. 1970)
5	Red	female	2	60	Rejected as hostile (University of Hawaii)
6	Al	male	2	65	Rejected as hostile (University of Hawaii)
7	Turk	female	3	95	Quick Find
8	Unknown	male	3	82	Rejected as unfit (University of Hawaii)
9	Unknown	male	3	69	Rejected as unfit (University of Hawaii)
10	Sniffer	male	1.5	45	Quick Find

This diagram from the NUC report shows the ten sea lions that were brought into the Quick Find selection process determining adaptability, suitability, and ability to learn the desired behaviors.

The report also stated that during training sessions, four California sea lions demonstrated the ability to locate and recover objects with pingers from a depth of 500 feet. In an actual system demonstration, they recovered an inert depth charge from 180 feet of water. The depth charge was 6 feet long and weighed approximately five hundred pounds, but the breakout force required to pull it out of the ocean bottom was greater than five hundred pounds. Recovery hardware was designed and fabricated that could be used by the sea lion to recover objects weighing approximately two thousand pounds.

The sea lions were selected, trained, and determined ready for a demonstration. There were two demonstrations planned for Maui, Hawaii, and San Nicholas Island (SNI), California. The Maui demonstration suffered several delays and was eventually canceled. That left one demonstration to be conducted at SNI by Naval Ammunition Depot (NAD) and Pacific Missile Range (PMR), Point Mugu using the U.S. Navy ship USS *Orleck*. The sea lions were trained to recover the ASROC MK 17 Depth Charge from 250 feet, with the ship firing the ASROC and the depth charge landing in 180 feet of water. The sea lions were shipped from Hawaii to California on October 26, 1971. There

Table 2. Training schedule of animal behaviors.

Average times are indicated.

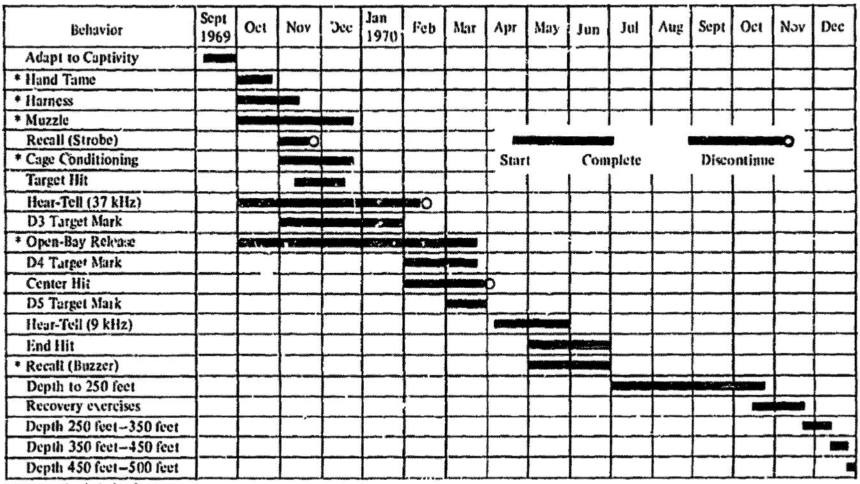

*Denotes basic behaviors.

The sea lion training schedule and behaviors.

Table 4. Training times from start to criterion.

Animal	Time[a]	* Hand Tame	* Harness	* Muzzle	Recall (Strobe)	* Cage Conditioning	Target Hit	Hear-Tell (37 kHz)	D3 Target Mark	* Open-Water Release	D4 Target Mark	Center Hit	D5 Target Hit	Hear-Tell (9 kHz)	End Hit	Recall (Buzzer)	Depth to 250 ft	Depth 250 to 500 ft[b]
No. 1 Akahi	hours	1:50	3:00	5:33	1:45	1:00	1:35	5:55	8:00	32:51	1:25	4:54	2:10	:43	7:50	:20	28:29	8:44
	calendar days	8	12	27	5	3	7	23	19	82	6	29	8	1	12	1	92	28
	training days	4	6	12	4	3	3	12	13	52	5	15	7	1	19	1	55	19
No. 2 Fatman	hours	2:50	14:45	4:12	:20	1:25	:20	12:36	:20	70:53	-	-	:20	2:50	8:02	1:30	25:29	12:00
	calendar days	21	105	161	1	9	1	122	1	152	-	-	5	3	21	3	92	28
	training days	7	32	22	1	7	1	33	1	108	-	-	2	3	14	3	55	19
No. 3 Sam	hours	1:15	2:40	3:30	2:30	:40	:60	6:04	7:10	41:03	2:00	4:48	4:00	:30	-	1:20	-	-
	calendar days	12	19	28	11	2	3	25	59	104	34	28	16	1	-	6	-	-
	training days	5	5	14	6	2	2	13	16	64	7	14	11	1	-	4	-	-
No. 4 Juneau	hours	-	-	-	1:40	-	2:10	5:54	:25	43:18	-	-	5:20	-	8:50	5:50	27:04	1:50
	calendar days	-	-	-	2	-	10	13	1	68	-	-	52	-	26	40	92	8
	training days	-[c]	-[c]	-[c]	2	-	4	12	1	40	-	-	10	-	17	11	53	6
No. 7 Turk	hours	0:35	-	:12	-	1:52	2	11:42	1	17:00	4:30	7:36	2:00	1	3:50	2:30	26:40	6:50
	calendar days	3	-	1	-	10	4	69	4	90	18	30	10	2	25	5	92	16
	training days	3	-	1	-	8	3	20	3	48	4	16	6	2	11	4	50	12
No. 10 Sniffer	hours	-	:20	1	-	1	:30	9:54	:30	29:50	:40	-	3:45	:15	13:50	7:20	33:30	8:57
	calendar days	-	1	5	-	2	1	47	1	72	2	-	14	1	36	50	92	26
	training days	-	1	3	-	2	1	29	1	44	2	-	11	1	27	18	52	17

* Denotes basic behaviors.

[a] Hours: Total time spent training from start of behavior to criterion.
Calendar Days: Total elapsed time from start to criterion.
Training days: Total number of days on which training took place

[b] Animal No. 4 deepest dive: 300 feet
Animal No. 7 deepest dive: 330 feet
Animal No. 10 deepest dive: 420 feet

[c] Behaviors previously conditioned at Point Mugu.

This diagram from the NUC report shows the sea lion training times in preparation for the project demonstration.

Above: Sam Ridgeway, Naval Undersea Center head veterinarian, was also known as the "Dolphin Doctor."

Right: The deep submergence vehicle "Alvin" was used to retrieve a nuclear weapon that had been lost in the sea due to an aircraft crash. The time and expense of this recovery mission inspired Sam Ridgeway to investigate other methods of retrieval.

were some weather delays and some technical difficulties, but the sea lions attached the grabber devices to the ASROC, and it was successfully recovered on November 6, 1971.

There is a story that Sam Ridgeway, then head veterinarian at NUC, also known as the "Dolphin Doctor," was surprised by the extensive time delay and expense it took to find a lost U.S. nuclear weapon in Spanish waters. The 1966 Palomares B-52 crash, or Palomares incident, occurred on January 17, 1966, when a B-52G bomber of the United States Air Force's Strategic Air Command collided with a KC-135 tanker during midair refueling at thirty-one thousand feet over the Mediterranean Sea, off the coast of Spain. The B52G carried four Mk28-type 1.45 megaton hydrogen bombs, of which three were found on land near the small fishing village of Palomares. The fourth, which fell into the Mediterranean Sea, was recovered intact after a two-and-a-half-month-long search. Apparently, it took the U.S. Navy an extraordinary amount of time and expense to transport the appropriate deep submergence vehicle (DSV) Alvin from the United States to Spain to search for the fourth nuclear weapon.

Sam, with his background in marine mammals, thought there had to be a better way to search for underwater objects. In fact, he had demonstrated use of a dolphin named Tuffy for carrying tools and messages between the

This page: Four nuclear bombs were recovered, three from land and one from sea, after a mid-air collision over the Mediterranean.

surface and the SEALAB II habitat two hundred feet below off La Jolla, California. Tuffy was also trained to locate and guide lost divers to safety and later, with another dolphin named Peg, was used in an ASROC recovery in 1967. So marine mammals had definitely demonstrated the capability.

The report ultimately recommended that "the sea lion recovery system should be used to augment existing recovery forces presently being used to recover experimental and test items."

Project Quick Find was born, and the program was moved from the Hawaii Laboratory to the Naval Amphibious Base (NAB) Coronado under the leadership of Torpedoman Chief (TNC) Gordon Sybrant. Chief Sybrant and more junior ranking marine mammal trainers EM2 John Busch and John Lemoyne were all Explosive Ordnance Disposal (EOD) qualified. Chief Sybrant was initially marine mammal trained in Kaneohe, Hawaii, by Don McSheehy, Mike Schultz, Milo McManus, and Jim Corey, all NUC civilian employees. Once they moved the program to California, they were first stationed in Point Magu, where they trained and demonstrated the sea lions' capabilities during a QAST (Quality Assurance Service Test)

Gordy's Quick Find Team and Plank Owners. *Top row, from left*: John Busch, Tom McHugh, Rick Hetzell. *Bottom row, from left*: Dan Peterson, Michael Wood.

demonstration at San Nicholas Island. Once they successfully completed that demonstration, they moved to Pier 13 at NAB Coronado.

It was unclear why more EOD personnel were not inducted into the project, but soon the call went out to recruit Navy SEAL personnel, many of whom were returning from operations in Vietnam. First amongst the SEALs to arrive was Bill Rosecrans, who served as a trainer and the only Navy SEAL for a while, but he needed to leave, and he recruited RM2 Richard Hetzell, who had just returned from deployment with SEAL Team One BRAVO Platoon. Next followed RM1 Thomas McHugh, and soon to follow him were PH2 Michael Wood and EN2 Dan Peterson, all of whom came from SEAL Team One. Although, Torpedoman Chief Sybrant ran the day-to-day operations, the recruiting process was under the guidance of LCDR Patterson, commander, Naval Inshore Warfare Command, Pacific.

Initially, there were five sea lions—Juneau, Turk, Sniffer, Fatman, and Akahi—that came from Hawaii, but by the time of my arrival there were only four, including Fatman, Akahi, Snitch, and the only female sea lion, Gump. Gordy Sybrant trained the most dominant animal, Fatman, and John Busch trained the next in line, Akahi. Both Akahi and Fatman were approximately the same size and weight, but Fatman had more of an attitude. Rick Hetzell initially trained Gump, the female, but soon inherited Snitch, the younger and smaller male sea lion. It was later determined through extensive training and testing that Gump would not ever measure up to be able to work during a missile recovery, so she was assigned to support any and all demonstrations for VIPs and news reporters. Gump's amiability with people and lack of ability to work on a missile recovery soon led to the decision to recruit or capture only male sea lions in the near future.

2
INDOCTRINATION

Upon my return from Vietnam, I was quickly assigned to another SEAL platoon. My new SEAL platoon was to deploy on a Western Pacific deployment traveling to several countries in the region to help train various foreign special forces instead of deploying back to Vietnam for real combat. What also made this platoon a bit strange was that SEAL Team One (ST1) assigned an Australian Special Air Service (SAS) officer as our platoon commander in an exchange program between Australia and the United States.

Our new platoon commander had not deployed to Vietnam, and he had a regimented leadership style. I started out training with the platoon as a point man, but I quickly learned that I was not interested at all in the new regimented training style, nor was I interested in training other foreign military. It was difficult to make the shift from the adrenaline-pumping combat missions in Vietnam back to a training environment to which I referred as "pretend operations."

I heard about a briefing that was taking place in the ST1 conference room having something to do with training sea lions. I did not know much about the program, but I wanted to find out. I have always had a strong interest in wild animals and nature, as well as nature photography. What I learned was that this group was called Project Quick Find and was looking for SEALs to transfer over to Naval Inshore Warfare Command (NIWC) to learn how to train California sea lions to recover inert anti-submarine rockets (ASROC). I did not know the first thing about training marine

Me in my point man war fighting gear, in front of the Victor Platoon barracks in Dong Tam, Vietnam, before transferring to Project Quick Find.

mammals, but I was highly intrigued and willing to learn. A couple of ST1 friends had already transferred over to Quick Find to work with Explosive Ordnance Disposal (EOD) Chief Petty Officer (CPO) Gordy Sybrant and Second Class Petty Officer John Busch. The ST1 friends who had previously transferred were Rick Hetzell and Tom McHugh. Both Dan Peterson and I attended the brief and signed up to transfer to Quick Find together. There were four of us SEALs working for an EOD CPO who ran the program and had actually brought Quick Find from Hawaii to Coronado, California. Chief Sybrant was already a seasoned veteran in the Quick Find project.

Sea lion training was only one small part of the program that we had to learn, and Chief Sybrant expected quick learning and mastery of the required skills. He did not tolerate any foolishness or lack of 100 percent effort. There was one tradition that might be considered foolishness that the chief did allow, and that was indoctrinating new trainers.

One of the most basic behaviors that the new trainer needed to learn was to "call" the selected sea lion to mount the dressing stand, where he would "harness the animal," or dress the animal by placing the harness over the sea lion's neck and connect the straps under and around his front pectoral flippers. This action forces the trainer to take his eyes off the sea lion while he is bending over to put the straps under and around the front flippers. It makes the trainer feel a bit exposed, with his neck right next to the animal's mouth and big teeth. This caused new trainers' sweat glands to exude a little fear!

If you have never seen the canines on a 70- to 120-pound male sea lion, they are very large, probably larger than any dog's, and sea lions are not afraid to show them. This, of course, sets up the "new guy" indoctrination by the older trainers. They, of course, call the sea lion to the stand and easily dress it in front of the new guy, showing the simple procedure.

Then they tell the new guy to call Fatman to the stand to dress him. It is unclear whether Fatman was in on the prank, but he sure played his role to perfection. The first thing the new trainer discovers is that Fatman does not respond immediately or at all to the signal of hand slapping the

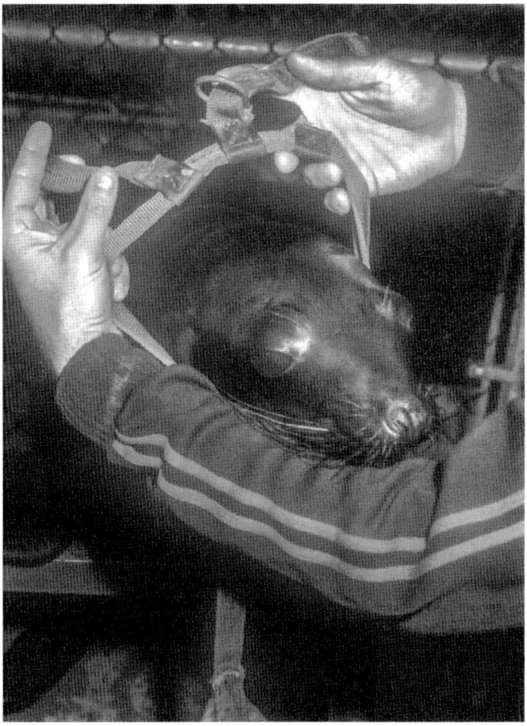

Left: Trainer Dan Peterson places the harness neck loop over the head of his sea lion.

Below: Trainer Bud Dennehy inspects Fatman's teeth while harnessing him on the dressing stand, with the sun setting over San Diego Bay in the background.

Opposite: A Project Quick Find trainer begins the process of harnessing a very large sea lion at the Naval Undersea Center.

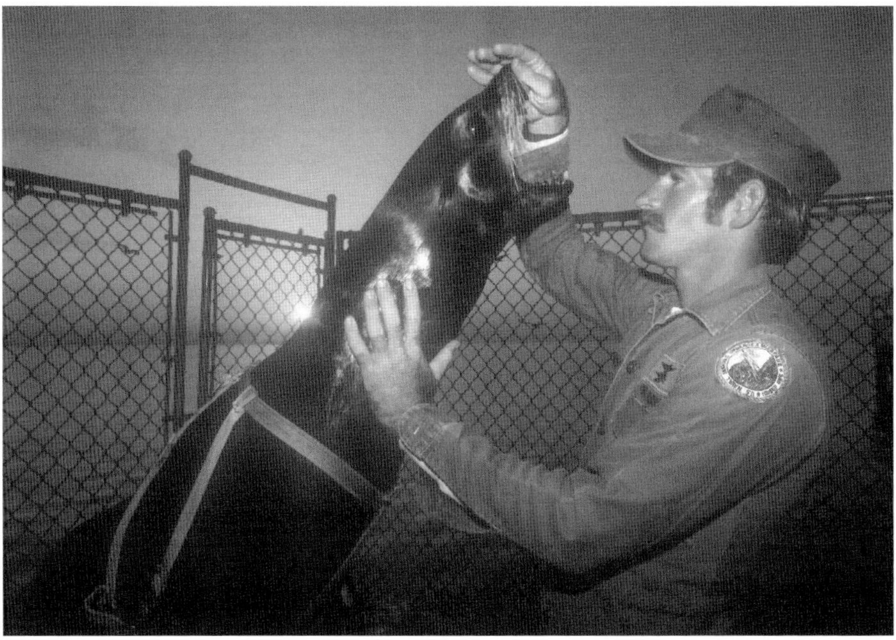

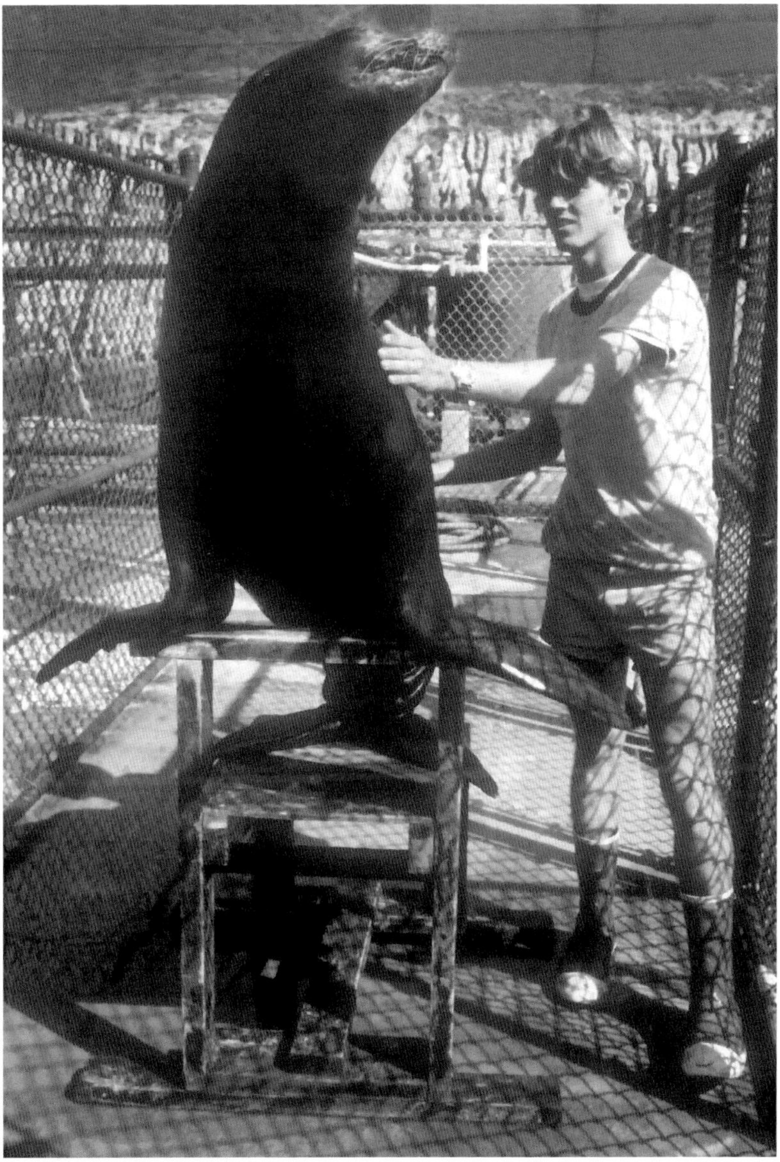

dressing stand. When the new guy saw the experienced trainers do that signal, the animal jumped right up on the dressing stand.

Fatman would just curl up his body and remain stationary on the deck and wasn't about to go anywhere. The new guy training did not cover what to do in case the sea lion didn't cooperate. In this instance, a newbie might think, "Well, I will just walk around Fatman and use my legs to nudge him

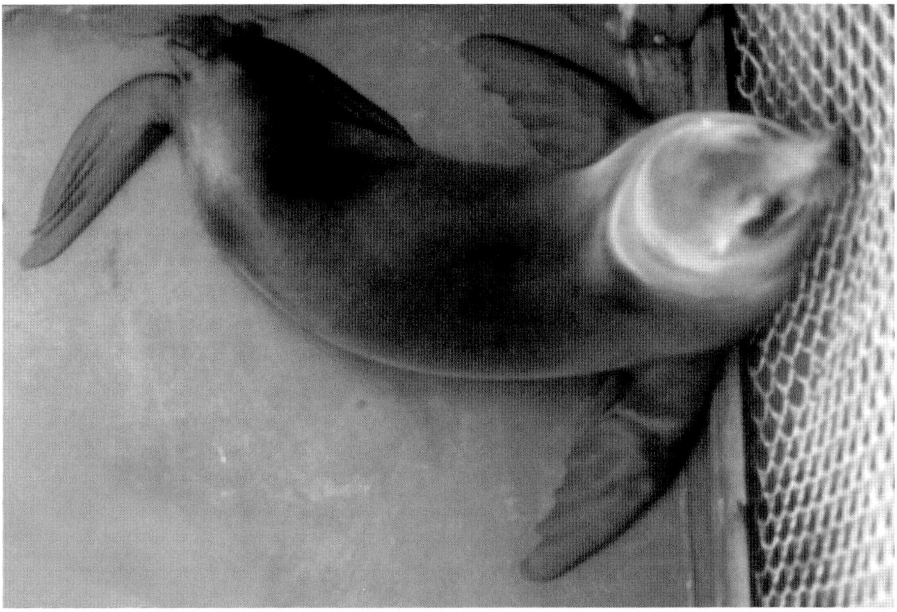

Fatman rests against the portable pen fencing on a navy ship during a QAST mission.

to the dressing stand." In my case, I am only five feet, four inches tall, and Fatman's head is about the same height as the top of my thighs and other important organs. So, as I tried to nudge Fatman with my leg to get him moving, his lightning speed head twisted, turned, and bent backward to strike and bite me right at my upper thigh, with his canines sinking fully into the meat just below other important parts. The strike was so quick I did not know it even happened until the delayed pain set in. Of course, the group of guys, including John Busch, Tom McHugh, and Rick Hetzell, were laughing their asses off. I wonder if they sold tickets for this scene.

Once you commit to a command with an animal, you have to see it through, so while bleeding from my thigh, I again slapped the dressing stand to call Fatman. He surprisingly jumped on the stand right away. Now, Fatman is equal to my eye level when he is on the stand, and he looked right into my eyes. He seemed to say, "Now you know who is the boss, and I will let you put the harness on me now!" With shaking hands, I placed the harness over Fatman's head and ran the straps around his flippers. I hooked up his walking strap to the harness, brought him down from the dressing stand, and handed him off to McHugh, who was waiting outside the pen to load Fatman into the barge cages. As I walked

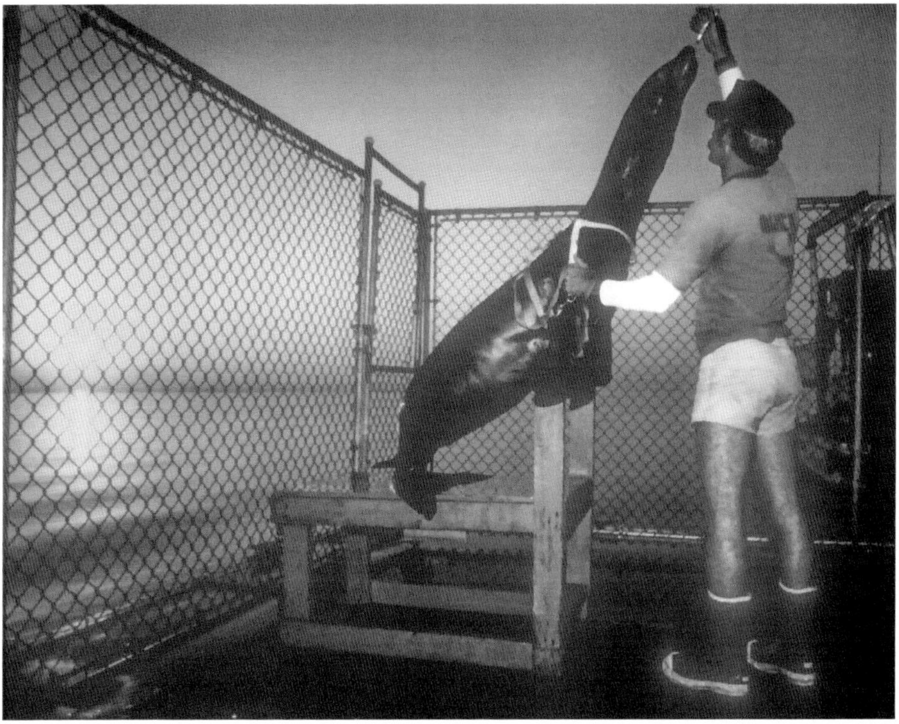

Trainer Bud Dennehy gives Fatman a reward of fish for getting harnessed on the dressing stand at the Quick Find pen in San Diego Bay.

out of the pen and past the laughter, a slight amount of shock was setting in, and I went right to the medical dispensary to get my tetanus shot and stitches. I learned a good lesson that day. Don't trust your SEAL buddies, and don't try to nudge the dominant animal with your legs.

Interestingly, I spent nine months operating as a SEAL point man in Vietnam without being wounded or earning a Purple Heart. A couple weeks of working with sea lions, and I get a sea lion bite wound. A tradition in the team is "payback is hell," and memories can last a long time.

3

ASROC RECOVERY

Project Quick Find was a new program and actually not fully accepted by the U.S. Navy. As a result, all the trainer and sea lion training occurred on the job, with no formal curriculum available. There were many skills to learn during this program, with very few people to do them all. This situation caused a need to learn quickly, which meant long working hours and lots of at-sea time. To understand what a new Quick Find trainer and sea lion needed to learn, one must first understand the ASROC locating and recovery process.

The navy had a requirement to periodically conduct a Quality Assurance Service Test (QAST) of the war reserve inventory of MK17 ASROC depth charges. Once an ASROC was selected from the war inventory in a bunker somewhere, the warhead was replaced with an instrument package to track the trajectory and other vital data needed for determining readiness of the ASROC war reserve inventory. The navy then selected a combatant ship and a missile range location where the test firing would occur. During my tenure at Quick Find, that generally occurred at San Clemente or San Nicholas Island in California; Little Creek or Norfolk, Virginia; or Mayport, Florida. Once the ship, site, and date were selected, the Quick Find team packed up all the necessary equipment and sea lion transport and housing gear and either transported by aircraft or transited by ship to the QAST test firing water area.

Part of the Quick Find duty was to set up the ASROC target radar reflector/buoy system in the selected water area prior to the ship firing the ASROC.

The navy periodically tests the war reserve inventory of MK17 ASROC depth charges from the war inventory.

Then, all ships and boat traffic were cleared from the firing area and confirmed by picket boats. That is why the missile firings were conducted in clearly defined military maritime areas. All clear, the selected ship would fire the ASROC, and typically it could be tracked by the naked eye, showing the launching plume to the splashdown in the water, resulting in a large but green splash and cloud of mist where the ASROC entered the water. The green came from the dye pack on the missile in order to aid Quick Find in locating the initial splashdown area. Our support ship or boat was typically about two miles away from the projected splashdown area, so our support ship/boat response time was delayed in reaching the area, and the green dye enabled us to follow the current or drift to the splashdown.

The goal was to reach the projected splashdown site and actually be within five hundred yards to a half mile from the real location. Once on site, we would launch our sixteen-foot Z-bird inflatable boat with a driver and pinger-receiver man. Each ASROC had a 9kz and 37kz pinger on the tail cone. The pinger man would listen for the 37 kHz signal with a receiver and headset to locate the ASROC and attempt to station the Z-bird directly over the top of the ASROC and drop a thirty-five-pound Danforth anchor and dual orange buoys to mark the location. There was at least one occasion when the ASROC 37 kHz had been detected and located from over a mile away by the pinger man, but that was out of the ordinary.

Tom McHugh drives the Z-bird and John Busch places the ASROC target radar reflector in the water prior to the navy ship firing the missile.

The ASROC missile launches from the navy ship in the missile range.

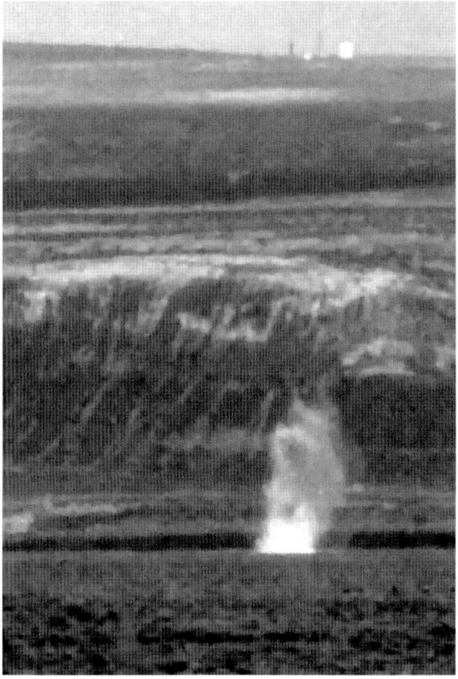

Left: The missile carried a green dye pack that exploded on impact with the water to aid in finding the initial splashdown area.

Right: Trainer Dan Peterson, wearing headphones, puts the pinger receiver over the side of the boat into the water to locate the 37 kHz pinger on the ASROC missile below.

Once the ASROC location is marked by the dual buoys, the Quick Find team of a sea lion, trainer, line handler, and boat driver load the Z-bird. They also bring a reel of five hundred feet of ⅜-inch Sampson braid line, a D-8 grabber device with a nose cone, and of course, a bucket of smelt for the sea lion reward.

The system for marking the ASROC missile below consisted of two orange buoys on the surface connected to the line. The first buoy marked the ASROC location below, and the second orange buoy trailed free, flowing with the current and indicating to the Z-bird driver which way the current was flowing. The Z-bird driver used this current indicator to drive the Z-bird up current about three to five boat lengths, where the boat driver would estimate to be located directly overhead of the target below or slightly up current of the target. This boat location gave the sea lion the best chance of locating the ASROC either visually or by listening for the 9 kHz pinger, which is in the sea lion's hearing range.

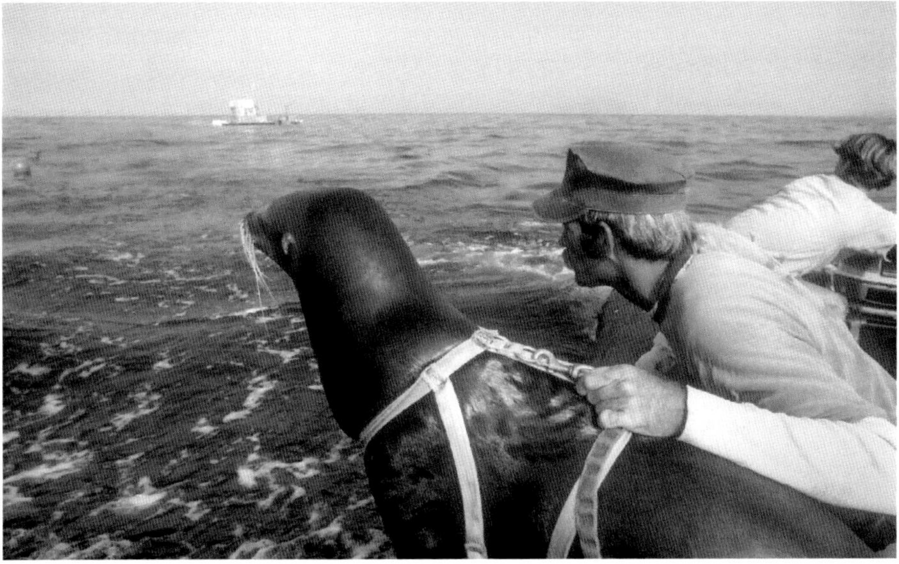

Once located, the site was marked by two orange buoys on the surface. Observations of the buoys' position and current flow allowed the boat driver to get in the best position for retrieval.

If the trainer was satisfied with the boat location, he would give the sea lion the hand signal to enter the water. The animal was typically raring to go by now and quickly entered the water and returned to the trainer, who would place the D8 or D9 grabber device with a nose cup over the nose and mouth of the animal. The sea lion then would quickly dive underwater and swim anywhere from 150 to 350 feet deep into the water depending on the depth of the ASROC. The missile would typically land almost in a vertical position, with its nose buried in the sand and the tail cone sticking straight up or at a slight angle.

The only indicator the trainer had of the sea lion's progress at this point was the speed at which the Sampson cord reel unwound as the sea lion kept swimming downward. All the sea lions have been trained to go at least five hundred feet deep and easily accomplish that depth. The water does get very cold and dark at that depth, and the sea lion may be relying totally on listening to the 9 kHz pinger to initially find the ASROC until it gets close enough to actually see it. Then, with the sea lion's very good sight in low light, the animal would place the D8 or D9 grabber device on the black section of the tail cone just under the rocket fins. The sea lion differentiates the fins and the cone shape due to the contrasting white and

Above and opposite: The sea lion was fitted with a grabber device over its nose and mouth. Once the sea lion located the missile, it would place the grabber device on the tail cone.

black stripes on the fin area. The sea lion would then place the grabber just under the rocket fins. Usually the sea lion would double-check the placement and then head back up to the surface.

As the sea lion placed the grabber, the small button on the grabber pushed in and released the spring-loaded circular arms that wrapped around the tail cone and locked in place. With the arms locked, the stainless steel small-diameter cable, which was attached to the Sampson cord, then tightened around the tail cone under the fins as the line was pulled to the surface.

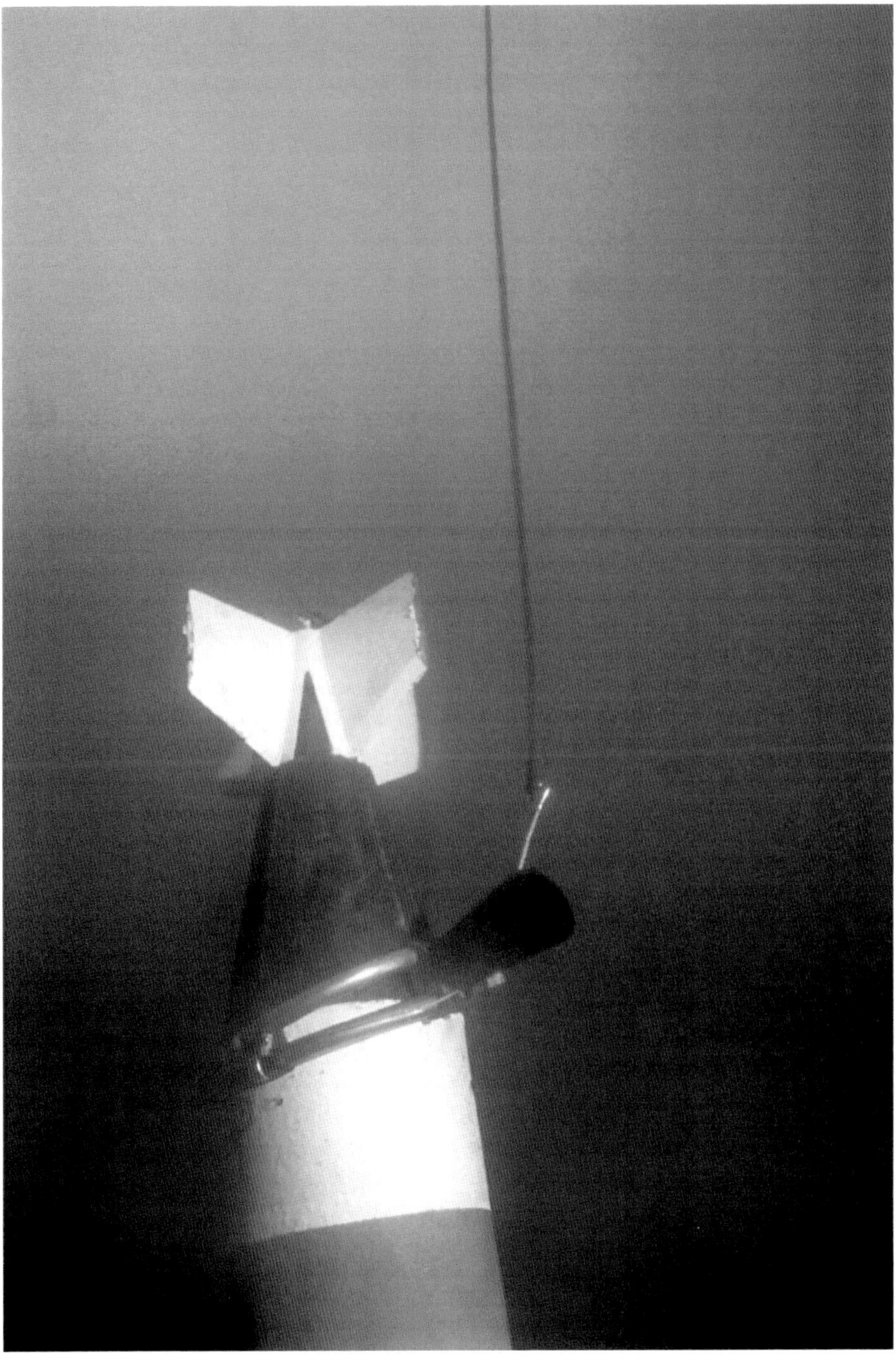

Above: The sea lion would double-check the placement of the grabber and then head back to the surface.

Right: Quick Find leading petty officer and trainer Tom McHugh communicates on the radio to the navy support craft, informing them the Z-bird rubber boat is returning home with the sea lion and crew. An ASROC is lifted out of the water in the background.

Trainer Mike Kelley, carrying a full bucket of fish, guides his sea lion back onto the navy support craft and to the portable pen following the successful ASROC recovery.

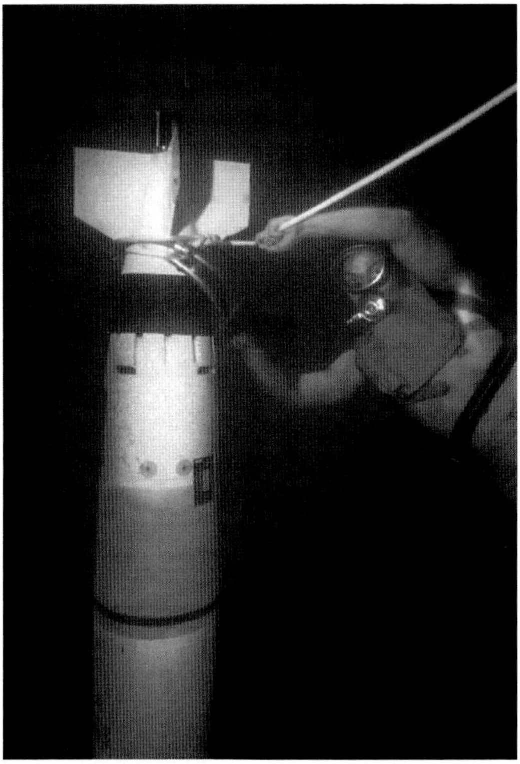

Left: A Quick Find scuba diver, approximately ten feet deep, places a 3/8-inch Sampson cord lifting line onto the ASROC tail cone and removes the D9 grabber devices to prevent damage to the grabber during final ASROC recovery.

Below: Chief Petty Officer Pat Gruber and Leading Petty Officer Tom McHugh maneuver the ASROC depth charge onto the deck of the navy landing craft utility (LCU), completing a successful ASROC recovery.

Here I am giving a five-gallon bucket of smelt to a sea lion following a successful QAST mission.

The sea lion did not waste any time swimming back up to the surface and usually jumped out of the water about a foot above the gunwale of the Z-bird and landed on the main tube next to the trainer. The line handler would take a strain on the line to determine if the grabber device was solidly connected to the ASROC. Then the trainer would reward the sea lion by hand-feeding it a few fish initially, but soon after he would let the sea lion dip his whole head into the bucket, wildly feeding on the five pounds of smelt. While the sea lion feeding frenzy continued, the Z-bird then drove toward the recovery ship, letting out the line as the ship and Z-bird closed distance.

The Z-bird driver would rendezvous with the ship and power the Z-bird nose into the ship, keeping it close without tying up lines. Once steady against the ship, the trainer and sea lion climbed over the bow of the Z-bird and onto the ship deck, walking directly to the portable pen where the sea lion would receive the rest of his fish reward. While that was going on, the line handler handed up the reel of line to personnel on deck of the recovery ship, usually right next to the crane or davit. The line would then be placed through the crane block and tackle and run to the winch, which was secured to the deck. The winch operator then took two to three wraps around the winch drum and started winching in the line, lifting the ASROC off the bottom. Winching up the three to five hundred feet of line took a while, but the ASROC would be lifted just below the surface of the water, where the winch operator held it in place as a scuba diver jumped in the water with another Sampson line and removed the grabber device from the tail cone to avoid damage to the close tolerance of the grabber mechanism. All the weight of the ASROC would now be transferred and lifted by the additional line, recovered on the deck of the support ship, and placed back into the shipping container.

4

GORDY'S TASK: TRAINING AND READINESS

The entire ASROC recovery process was much more complex than first appearances indicated. The entire process needed to be broken down into incremental training steps for both the trainer and the sea lion. The trainer training cycle would be accomplished in a couple of months, but for the sea lion, it would take from six to nine months.

Chief Gordon Sybrant had a difficult task at hand. He had upcoming QAST recoveries soon to be tasked by the navy but he also had a project that just recently moved locations and a group of four out of six trainers who were new and had to be trained in a short period of time without any formal training program or support and with limited equipment. That was the challenge for Gordy. He had two out of three sea lions QAST recovery ready, so all he had to do was use his two experienced trainers to get the other four up to speed while maintaining the training of the existing experienced sea lions.

We started going to sea about two to three miles off Point Loma, totaling a twenty-four- to twenty-eight-mile round-trip transit, plus the five to six hours of at-sea training time, every day five to six days a week come rain or shine. We had an old thirty-six-foot work barge with dual 115hp Evinrude outboard motors (OBM) to make the transit, and it seemed we were always fixing the motors and plowing through waves not only in San Diego harbor but also transiting in the five- to six-foot swells off the coast of Point Loma.

Left: Chief Gordon Sybrant.

Below: Chief Petty Officer Gordy Sybrant demonstrates how to drive the Z-bird and simultaneously listen on the pinger receiver for the mock-ASROC target 37 kHz pinger below, as John Busch and Tom McHugh observe.

On one occasion, we had only one operational starter for the two 115hp outboard motors, and we would start one motor, remove the starter, and put it on the other OBM and start it; if one OBM stopped, we would have to repeat the process. We even got towed out to sea one time because none of the OBMs were working. Nothing stopped at-sea training, not equipment casualties or sea states. Many times, boats were returning to port due to small-craft warnings, and there we were limping out to sea to train.

The plan was for John Busch and Tom McHugh, our leading petty officer, to place each of us (Peterson, Hetzell, and me) in the various positions needed to train the animals every day. We had to learn how to drive the barge, drive the Z-bird, maneuver the Z-bird to the best position in line with the buoys to

This page: The training barge heading out to Point Loma for training exercises.

Tom McHugh drives the Z-bird, lining up with buoys, while Rick Hetzell readies the training grabber device. John Busch gets sea lion Akahi ready for a training dive off Point Loma, California.

launch the sea lion over the target, operate the winch, serve as line handler, launch and recover the training target, handle the sea lions in and out of their barge cages, prepare the fish, and perform many other at-sea training duties. As the days and weeks passed, we each became proficient in these basic duties and eventually were able to switch and take one another's duties when required. Once we showed proficiency in those duties, as well as duties required when ashore, we started cycling in and learning each of the phases to handle the sea lions.

We started with the very basic animal behavior duties, such as signaling the sea lions to come out of the water, placing them in their individual pens with tubs, calling the animals to the dressing stand, harnessing the sea lions on the dressing stand, walking the animals from the floating pen to their cages on the barge, putting the animals in and out of their cages, and walking the animals to the Z-bird while alongside the barge at sea.

As we learned how to perform these basic animal behavior functions, Gordy would eventually start letting us handle the animals in the Z-bird and put them through their diving behaviors at sea. That, of course, was the most fun, working with the sea lions in the Z-bird inflatable rubber boat. The trainer would be in the front of the boat on the bow with the sea lion's front flippers standing on the bow gunnel right next to the trainer, and many times the sea conditions would knock the sea lion into the trainer as the boat bounced up and down. This would sometimes make it difficult for the trainer to give the driver directions to align the boat with the target buoy lines.

The pictures on this page all illustrate the succession of naive animal training behaviors that must be accomplished before graduating to at-sea training. Here I am at left leading a sea lion into the portable pen on the navy LCU after training for an ASROC recovery.

Left: I walk my sea lion Sinbad from the thirty-six-foot work barge deck onto the Z-bird inflatable boat for training out at sea off Point Loma, San Diego.

Right: Trainer Dan Peterson demonstrates how to harness a sea lion on the dressing stand. He keeps the sea lion's attention with one hand while connecting the harness belly strap as the animal waits patiently on the stand.

These were trained sea lions, so they were never tethered during at-sea training. The animals could take off any time they wanted, but I soon learned that the sea lions seemed to prefer the short amount of work they had to do everyday, diving to earn the five to ten pounds of smelt and mackerel we fed them.

Sinbad has graduated to at-sea training. Here I am about to have him dive and mark a mock-ASROC target on the bottom off of Port Loma, almost the same location where he was originally found as a hungry pup. The work barge can be seen in the background.

The rest of the time, they just sunned themselves or swam in their pool. I guess in a sea lion's mind that would be preferable to hunting for their daily food, having to swim long distances in the ocean where predators might be waiting for them.

Hard work at sea was not all we did. There was plenty of work and training back at our compound at Pier 13 on the Naval Amphibious Base (NAB) in Coronado, California. Our compound was a classic example of the navy support to Project Quick Find in the early days.

Our building was an old and rustic World War II Quonset hut that was built when NAB was first established for training World War II navy personnel. The floating pen that we used to house the animals alongside Pier 13 was beginning to fall apart, with floating barrels sinking, and our thirty-six-foot work barge needed extensive maintenance to keep it going.

Some of the "most fun" (sarcasm) were trainer house-keeping duties to daily scrub down the pen decks and tubs with strong but diluted disinfectant cleaner and to periodically clean the nets hanging in the water that form a community pool for the sea lions. The disinfectant cleaner was strong so

Sea lions Akahi and Snitch lean against the portable pen net and rest in the sun after a full day of training onboard a navy LCU.

Dan Peterson thaws out the day's fish ration in a stainless-steel tub near the edge of the Quick Find facility quay wall, located at Pier 13 on the Naval Amphibious Base in Coronado, California. The Quick Find building, an ancient World War II quonset hut, can be seen in the background, and the original portable pen on a trailer is in the foreground next to the quay wall.

we diluted it significantly and wore rubber boots when in the pen. Daily cleaning was required because the sea lions were not too concerned about where they left their calling cards, whether in the water, on the deck, or on and in their tubs. Their excrement was greasy and pungent. Just ask our wives, who would make us take our sea lion training clothes off outside before we could come into the house.

One time when cleaning the decks during a Sunday duty watch, I was in a hurry and did two things that weren't too smart. First, I did not dilute the disinfectant and poured it directly on the deck straight from the bottle. Second, I cleaned the pens while barefoot because I had forgotten my rubber boots. I did thoroughly rinse the deck down afterward of the disinfectant residue so it would not affect the animals.

That night, I learned the error of my ways. By the time it was bedtime, I had noticed the entire top of both of my feet were covered in what looked like a hive of tiny blister bubbles. There were blister bubbles on top of bubbles, all of which were filled to their individual capacity with fluid. Within each individual bubble, there was a corresponding pinpointed intense itch. I used all of my Navy SEAL willpower to not scratch or pop the blisters. I knew that was bad. About three o'clock in the morning, I jumped out of bed, went to the bathtub, filled it a quarter full with water, and then poured a gallon of bleach into the tub and mixed it. Then I grabbed a new and clean scouring pad and scraped off the hive of blisters

The original home for the Quick Find sea lions was a floating pen. It consisted of three separate cages with tubs for water, a common deck, and a community pool, surrounded by a chain-link fence, floating on fifty-five-gallon drums tied alongside Pier 13. A Z-bird is seen here tied up to the pen.

on the top of my feet. Blister fluid oozed everywhere, and the pain made my eyes squint tightly closed. Then I enacted my most brilliant idea of putting my raw-skin feet into the tub of bleach water. To say the pain was intense would be an understatement. That said, the intense pain was a wonderful, wonderful relief from the previous intense itching. I know that was a stupid thing to do, especially with the potential for infection. The burning pain persisted as I rinsed my feet in the faucet, running fresh water. Though the pain persisted, I was now able to go to sleep finally for the first time that night. By morning, the blisters were dried up and gone, no more itch, and the top of my feet began to scab over and the pain subsided. Luckily, I did not get an infection, and I definitely learned my lesson to always wear my rubber boots when cleaning the pens.

The other "very fun" housecleaning task was to clean the marine growth or fouling off the floating pen pool netting in the San Diego Bay water. Anyone who cleans boat bottoms knows the extensive marine growth and fouling that can grow during the summer months in the bay water. Here is what a report on marine fouling in San Diego Bay by John Conway and Loren Locke in 1994 says: "Fouling refers to the growth of various marine organisms on submerged surfaces. Fouling organisms commonly found in San Diego Bay include the tube-building polychaete worms or tubeworms, encrusting bryozoans or moss animals, algae, small sponges, tunicates, barnacles, and other sessile organisms (Johnston, 1990). Fouling can be seen on any surface that has been submerged in the bay for ten days or more, and can grow to a substantial build if left undisturbed for a prolonged period of time."

This type of marine growth, or fouling, would grow on the floating barrels supporting the pen and the sea lions' pool netting. The marine organisms would consist of tube-building polychaerte worms, tube worms, encrusting bryozoans, moss animals, algae, small sponges, and barnacles. We just collectively called them "nookie nows."

We just called them "nookie nows." They could get very large and hang deep, looking like a mixture of upside-down weeds, grass, and kelp pods without the leaf blades. Inside each of the look-alike kelp pods, which were translucent, you could see little wiggling creatures that looked like miniature models from the alien movies. We would scuba dive or snorkel wearing wetsuits in the water to clean the fouling off the nets. Once we disturbed the "nookie nows," it seemed like we were massively attacked by a swarm of miniature hook-armed body snatchers. Once the nets were clean, we would get out of the water and try to clean our wetsuits of the hundreds of little hook-armed monsters caught in the tiny mesh of our wetsuit material.

As nasty as some of the housecleaning duties sound, we loved every minute of it. Among our many duties, we also designed and built another floating pen for the animals that was larger, had more tubs and pens, and had its foundation on a large multi-pontoon hull that was stable, secure, and water transportable and a vast improvement on the flooding and rusty fifty-gallon barrels the old pen was built on. We also installed new and clean netting for the animal community pool. No more "nookie nows" for a while.

Finally, we also had to haul the thirty-six-foot work barge out of the water to overhaul and refurbish the entire barge. This included sanding off the old red lead hull paint. We were not aware of lead paint dangers in those days. We scraped and sanded down the barge hull

The newly built floating pen and home for the sea lions, built by Quick Find personnel. This pen was built on a much more stable pontoon boat with more individual animal cages and tubs, a larger common deck space, and a community netted pool. Unlike the old pen's fifty-five-gallon drums, the pontoons would not flood and could be towed to new locations if required.

Fatman trainer and Quick Find leading petty officer Tom McHugh drives the Z-bird at sea.

without wearing any respiratory or face masks. We soon learned how caustic the red lead paint was when all of us got burning eyes and serious chest congestion, but we finished the barge hull repainting. Add that hazardous duty to the breathing in of the paint fumes from painting the entire barge top to bottom and I guess you could say we earned our extra fifty dollars a month of hazardous duty pay, which was really for parachuting and demolition duty hazards.

It was during this work period that the idea of "payback" occurred to me. I did blame Tom McHugh for the Fatman biting incident because he was one of Fatman's trainers. He knew Fatman's behaviors, plus he made the training assignments. While refurbishing the barge, we needed more haze grey paint for the barge cabin and trim, and we asked Tom to grab a gallon of the grey from the paint locker.

Some industrious young petty officer with a long memory had planted a pile of human feces in one of the empty haze grey gallon cans and placed it strategically in the paint locker about two weeks earlier. That gallon can sat in a small paint locker exposed to the summer sun for about two weeks. I am not a physicist, but I can imagine the sun and heat effect on the contents of the closed-up gallon can. Tom went to the paint locker and grabbed the first gallon can of haze grey that he saw. He did not notice the slightly bulging walls of the can. Luckily, he brought the can out of the paint locker before he tried to open it to check the paint contents. He was quite visible to all of us, as we were painting the barge several feet away. All it took was the slightest pressure from the head of the flathead screwdriver he used to pry open the lid and *POW*! The lid went flying, the buildup of methane gas rapidly escaped directly upward, and the can's ingredients exploded in tiny chocolate-colored bits all over Tom's face and body. The laughter that immediately followed was much more raucous than the laughter during my Fatman biting incident. Our painting work

The haze gray paint provided an opportunity for some much-deserved prank payback—as well as being a good color for the barge.

on the barge continued without skipping a beat but at a much faster pace. Tom never did figure out who was the paint can perpetrator. He might after this book comes out, though.

Gordy, John Busch, and Tom McHugh remained the prime trainers, especially for QAST missions, but Peterson and Hetzell were beginning to work occasionally with Fatman and Akahi and training Snitch preparing him for QAST shots. Gump was always a good standby sea lion for a trainer to learn all the animal handling steps. I filled in on all the various positions as required and would later find a specialized duty with naïve animal training. I think the larger sea lions were prejudiced against us vertically challenged people.

All joking aside, my smaller stature next to the larger sea lions when in the bouncing Z-bird boat did seem to concern Gordy, so I was not selected as a primary trainer. One must be able to handle and control the 80- to 120-pound aggressive sea lions in a small, sixteen-foot rubber boat bouncing around while transiting in up-to-sea-state-three conditions. Not being a primary trainer ended up being a blessing in disguise. It actually freed me up to be the photographer for the group, which fit in nicely with my previous Photographer's Mate "A" School training that I received right before leaving SEAL Team One. This also later had a significant benefit to my future application for the Military Photojournalism Program at Syracuse University. It was my Project Quick Find portfolio that helped with the navy selecting me for that program. I learned that all things work together for good.

Although I was not a primary trainer, I was a primary QAST team member and participated in all of our ASROC recovery missions. Gordy

Quick Find Plank Owners! *Left to right*: Tom McHugh, Gordon Sybrant, Michael Wood, Rick Hetzell, and Dan Peterson. John Busch is absent from the photo.

managed to put together a fully trained and functional team of trainers and sea lions in a short six-month period, and we were ready for the soon-to-come QAST missions.

5
QAST SHOTS

QAST is an acronym for Quality Assurance Service Test, and during my tenure we seemed to participate in a QAST about every six months on the East or West Coast. This is how Project Quick Find earned its keep.

The sponsoring military activity was the Naval Ordnance Systems Command in Washington, D.C. Initially, the plan for the sea lions was to be an effective alternative to the use of divers and submersibles for underwater recovery of various objects lost at sea, including exercise mines, torpedoes, or aircraft and not just ASROC missiles. Once the Naval Undersea Research and Development Center submitted the final assessment and report of Project Quick Find in June 1972, the sponsoring military activity began planning the QAST schedule.

Participating in a QAST shot was like qualifying for the Olympics. We trained and trained and trained, and when a QAST would be announced, it was so exciting to be able to put all that training to the real test and obtain the ultimate goal of recovering an ASROC missile. There was definitely a feeling of accomplishment after a successful recovery. We had other brethren back at the base in what was then called Project Short Time who were training dolphins to locate and mark swimmers. It seemed at the time that their project would train forever without ever being able to put it to a real time test, so we felt lucky to be able to demonstrate the sea lions' capabilities. There was some competition between the dolphin and sea lion trainers in the marine mammal program at the time.

Tom McHugh drives the Z-bird, Rick Hetzell handles the reel of a grabber line, and John Busch places a D5 training grabber on Akahi's nose while training at sea.

During the next two-year period, Project Quick Find conducted at least four QAST missions and I believe more but I can't document them. This was a time when the three working sea lions and the six trainers were a well-oiled team and, for the next two years, would prove the success of the project.

The QAST missions that I can document occurred in June and September 1974 and then in June and July 1975 at San Nicholas Island, California; Little Creek and Norfolk, Virginia; and Mayport, Florida.

On one of the Florida QAST missions, there was one interesting experience that happened while training out at sea in the Gulf of Mexico.

We were putting Akahi through his pre-QAST training, and John Busch hand signaled for him to enter the water. Akahi enthusiastically did so and quickly took the D5 training grabber from John to start his dive. Suddenly, and much sooner than expected, Akahi returned and launched out of the water at least a full body length above the boat, dropping with a thud onto the boat deck, not the main tube. His eyes were uncharacteristically wide open. I was the Z-bird driver at the time, and just as Akahi dove in the water, I did notice two very large and dark-looking manta rays gliding under us about twenty feet down. I did not think much about the harmless

Akahi wasted no time jumping out of the water when spooked by manta rays swimming by.

filter feeders going by, but Akahi apparently did not like those large dark shapes moving right under where he was diving. Dominant male sea lions are not usually that intimidated, but apparently large dark shapes in the water can cause that reactive response.

Florida QAST shots also stand out in my memory because the first time we took the animals to Florida in June 1974, unknown to us, the sea lions were exposed to and bitten by Florida mosquitoes. The results of those mosquito bites manifested several months later, with one of our sea lions, Snitch, dying. The autopsy showed that his heart was loaded with heartworms. I was there for that autopsy, and I can say that his heart was completely filled with worms. I am not sure how his heart was able to pump any blood at all. This led to an effort by veterinarians at the Naval Undersea Center (NUC) to put the rest of our sea lions (Fatman and Akahi) that went to Florida through a heartworm treatment program. That was to be a very ugly period for the animals.

The treatment required the introduction of arsenic into the animals' blood system. That really had us all very worried because the treatment was almost worse than the disease itself. The arsenic would either kill the sea lions or kill the worms. I will say that the autopsy showed these were not little inchworms that were in Snitch's heart. The worms were anywhere from three to six inches long, so I can see how that drastic treatment was required. Snitch was the smallest of the male sea lions, so we believe that contributed to his death. Both Fatman and Akahi were a good twenty pounds heavier than Snitch. We knew the medical treatment was going to be rough so we transferred them to the NUC facility on Point Loma so they would be continually observed and under the constant care of the veterinarians. Due to Fatman and Akahi's size, we also needed the NUC squeeze cage to hold the animals so we could draw

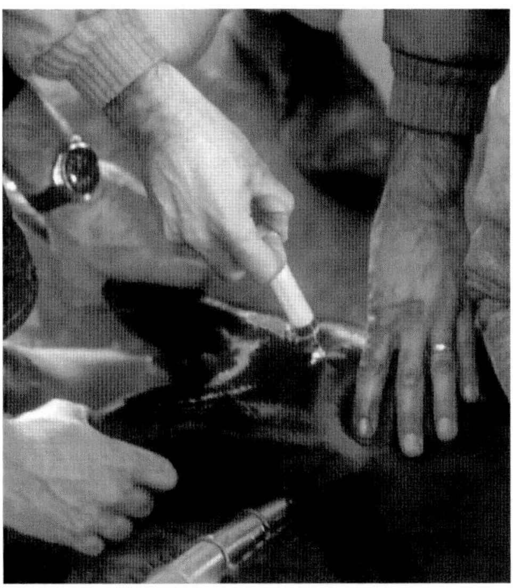

NUC veterinarians draw a blood sample from a sea lion. The treatment for heartworms was a very ugly period for Fatman and Akahi.

blood and administer the medication. A trainer can hold a moderate-sized sea lion down by kneeling over his back and tucking his pectoral flippers in under his body, essentially pinning him down. This technique would never work with the larger and dominant sea lions such as Fatman and Akahi. There were no humans big enough to hold Fatman or Akahi down like that, so we used the squeeze cage, which is about five feet tall and four feet wide with two-inch tubular bars spaced alternately on each side and curving upward to a point. As the top of the cage was lowered, the alternating bars essentially pinned the sea lion to the deck of the cage without risking injury to any human or to the animal. I do not remember how long the treatment took, but I remember it happened at least for a couple of weeks where the sea lions were getting arsenic shots on a daily basis. The treatment seemed to make the sea lions lethargic and sensitive to surrounding noises. Thankfully, both sea lions survived the treatment and, after a few weeks of downtime, were ready to get back into training and going to sea. Our lesson learned from that experience was to put the sea lions through a heartworm treatment procedure prior to conducting a QAST shot on the East Coast and especially Florida.

Now that the animals were healthy again and up to speed on their training, we were ready for the next QAST, which was scheduled for

The squeeze cage was used to hold down larger sea lions that a human could not safely control for blood work and treatment.

September 1974 at San Nicholas Island (SNI) in California. The next QAST was close to home so the animals did not have to travel far. In fact, we transited by boat at sea from San Diego to San Nicholas Island.

The USS *William V. Pratt*, DDG 44, a Farragut-class destroyer, was scheduled to fire the ASROC in the missile range off San Nicholas Island. This location was good because it was our home turf. We were there for six days and conducted some training prior to the shot to get the animals acclimated to the San Nicholas waters.

Once the firing ship was on station, we placed the target radar reflector at the designated coordinates, and all boat traffic was cleared from the area. We did have some VIPs attend this QAST to observe the process.

Above: The USS *William V. Pratt* fired the ASROC missile for the QAST mission off San Nicholas Island.

Opposite, top left: Tom McHugh inspects the ASROC radar reflector target and float prior to emplacement.

Opposite, top right: An ASROC radar reflector target is placed a couple of miles off the coast of San Clemente Island.

Opposite, middle: The USS *William V. Pratt* (DDG-44), a Farragut-class destroyer, fires the ASROC missile.

Opposite, bottom: Green dye and smoke show how close the ASROC landed to the radar reflector target. Quick Find will use the smoke and dye to conduct the initial pinger receiver search for the missile.

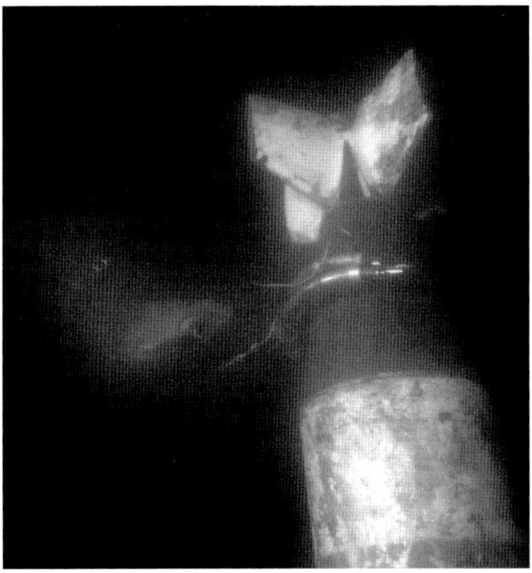

Above: Akahi jumps out of the water and onto the gunwale of the Z-bird next to trainer John Busch to get his fish reward after successfully attaching the grabber to the ASROC.

Left: A sea lion correctly places the D9 grabber onto the mock-ASROC tail cone.

The ship fired the ASROC on schedule, and we watched the fire from about two miles away and were able to visually track it through the air and splashdown in the water near SNI. This time, we did see the splashdown and the resulting green mist rising in the air. We then transited to the splashdown site and used the green dye trail to reach the Z-bird launch site.

Once on site, we launched the rubber boat with a line, anchor, and floats, as well as a handler and a pinger receiver operator to narrow down the ASROC bottoming-out point. Detection and location did not take long, and before we knew it, the Z-bird was back to the support boat to pick up the sea lion, trainer, and necessary gear.

The trainer and sea lion loaded into the Z-bird. The green dye was beginning to fade in the current flow, but we now had the two orange buoys to indicate the ASROC location.

SNI shoreline and water depth drops down quickly, so this particular ASROC firing ended up in a little deeper water, nearing at least three hundred feet deep. The Z-bird driver lined the boat up, and the trainer sent the sea lion into the water. There was great anticipation with every sea lion dive because locating the missile was never a sure thing. This was where lining up the boat correctly can play a big role in a successful contact for the sea lion. On the first dive, the line handler recovered the line, and the D8 grabber had not fired. No fish reward for the sea lion. The trainer had the boat driver go a little farther up current and sent the sea lion back into the water. Again, the grabber came back to the surface. You never really know what currents the sea lion has to deal with at the different depths. The trainer decided to check the location with the pinger receiver, and the boat location seemed to be correct. He launched the sea lion again. This time, once the line stopped reeling out, the line handler took a strain, and the line pulled taut, indicating the grabber had grasped the ASROC. This time when the sea lion surfaced, he got his full fish reward.

Above and next page: Despite a large grey-colored piece obscuring the white tail fins, the sea lion still attached the grabber to complete the mission.

The rest of the ASROC recovery went as normal until it neared the surface and became visible. This time there was a grey-colored section still attached above the top of the rocket fins. The diver entered the water, attached the additional lifting line, and removed the D8 grabber. The ASROC was recovered on deck and placed in the shipping container. Apparently the grey-colored section that separates the depth charge from the rocket motor that lifts the ASROC did not separate as usual and remained on the ASROC. The amazing thing is the rocket motor

ASROC missile sits on the deck of the navy LCU, showing that the rocket motor did not separate from the depth charge portion of the missile. The presence of two sets of fins had potential to confuse the sea lions in placing the grabber device.

section completely obscured the white tail fins. The sea lion still placed the grabber onto the white below the grey/black section of the rocket even though the fins were not visible. I guess the sea lion decided that his third dive to three hundred feet was enough and placed the grabber on the ASROC as trained without seeing the fins. The sea lion did not want to come up unrewarded for a third time. The grey section rocket motor did significantly change the overall appearance, but the sea lion adapted and overcame.

There were two other QAST shots in Virginia where one was based out of NAB Little Creek and another based out of Norfolk. These QASTs ended successfully, just as the California and Florida shots. It seemed as if the QAST shots in Virginia and Florida attracted the most news media attention.

Chief Sybrant usually handled most of the news media requests, but occasionally whoever was the current officer-in-charge (OIC) would address the media. There was always interest from the public about what the navy was doing with sea lions. Some of this public interest was natural curiosity, and occasionally there was the search by the media to find the killer dolphin or killer sea lion conspiracy. Project Quick Find was always an open source unclassified project for the simple purpose of recovering objects from the ocean floor. Sometimes there was a little news media disappointment in the benign purpose of the project. Most often, though, it was just natural curiosity about the sea lions and how

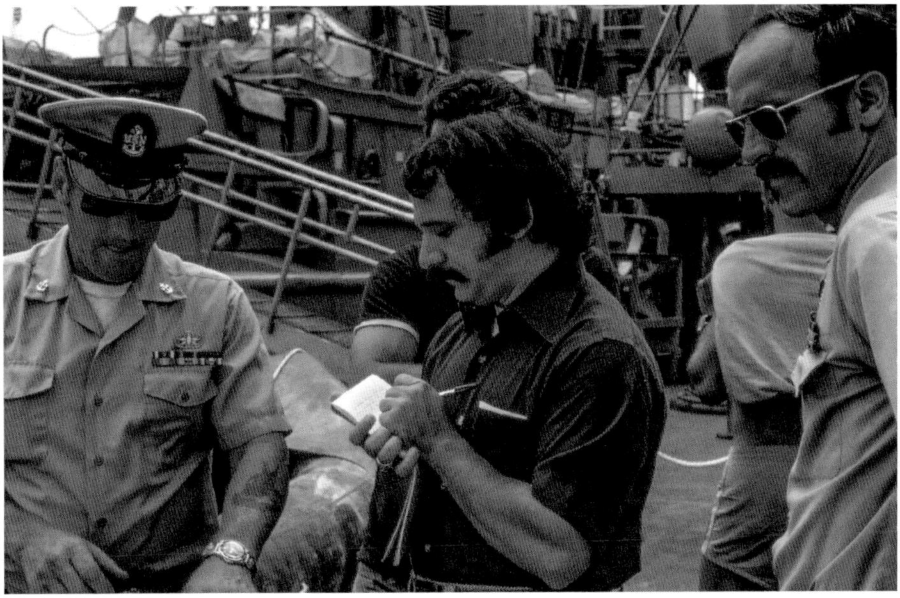

This page: Chief Gordon Sybrant and OIC LT Paul Plumb review and explain Quick Find equipment to reporters and VIPs in Norfolk, Virginia.

Occasionally we would have time to play hard, like this visit to a go-cart track in Little Creek.

they behaved and whether or not they loved their trainers. Many times we would put on a trainer and sea lion display, sort of like a mini Sea World demonstration.

Sometimes, though, all was not just hard work. Occasionally we would have time to play hard just like we worked hard. One late evening, I do remember a trip into town for a little imbibing and then a visit to a go-cart attraction in Little Creek. Most of the guys were fairly sober, but there was one young SEAL in the group who had a bit too much to drink. We were the only ones on the go-cart track, and the whole group enjoyed racing around, passing each other, and ramming into each other like little kids—this included the chief, although ramming of the carts was forbidden.

That evening, the youngest member of the group had severely impaired his prefrontal cortex, which controls inappropriate social behavior. He really did not want to quit driving the go-cart when he saw the flagman waving the flag for the "one more lap" signal and then again for the "return the cart" signal. A brilliant idea occurred to the young SEAL. That is always a dangerous thing, both from an alcohol standpoint but also from an age maturity standpoint. The great idea persisted, and the young SEAL swerved around the flagman and continued driving around the go-cart course with the flagman chasing behind. As he was about to complete the unauthorized lap, another bright idea occurred just about the time that the flagman had reinforcements to stop the go-cart driver. Bushes surrounded the go-cart facility perimeter with openings to the adjacent public street. "Why not drive around these guys and take the go-cart for a ride on the street?" he brilliantly thought. "That should be fun!" No sooner had the thought entered his mind than he put it into action and quickly swerved around the multiple flagmen, driving the go-cart through the foliage opening and onto the dark

Gordy Sybrant stands on the bow ramps of the LCU support craft and looks out to sea toward the target area.

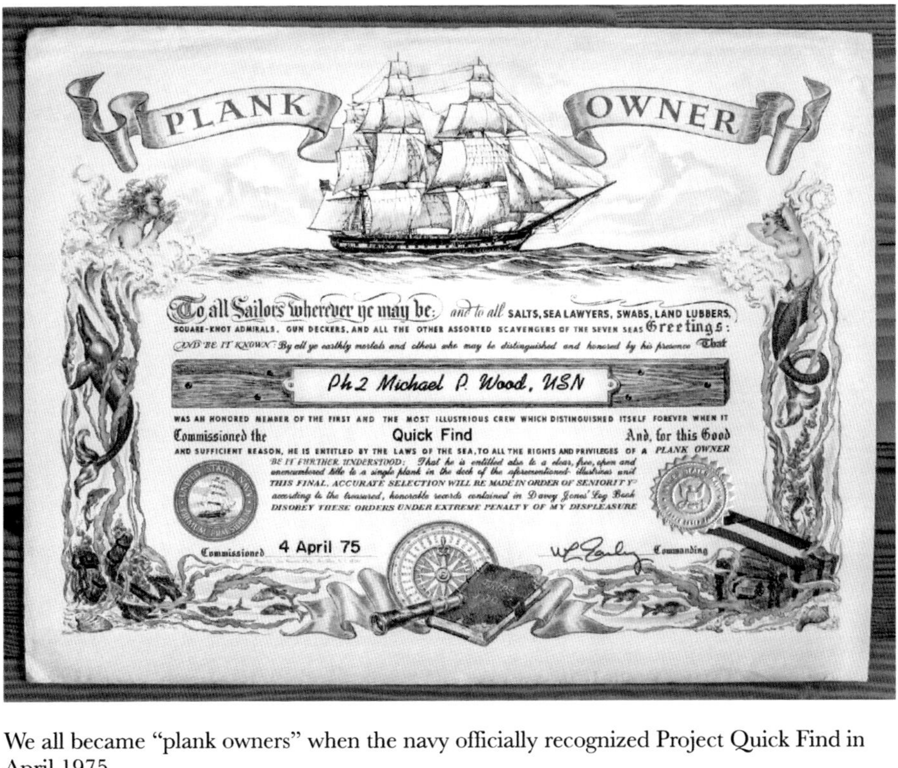

PLANK OWNER

To all Sailors wherever ye may be: and to all SALTS, SEA LAWYERS, SWABS, LAND LUBBERS, SQUARE-KNOT ADMIRALS, GUN DECKERS, AND ALL THE OTHER ASSORTED SCAVENGERS OF THE SEVEN SEAS Greetings:

AND BE IT KNOWN: By all ye earthly mortals and others who may be distinguished and honored by his presence That

Ph2 Michael P. Wood, USN

WAS AN HONORED MEMBER OF THE FIRST AND THE MOST ILLUSTRIOUS CREW WHICH DISTINGUISHED ITSELF FOREVER WHEN IT Commissioned the Quick Find And, for this Good AND SUFFICIENT REASON, HE IS ENTITLED BY THE LAWS OF THE SEA, TO ALL THE RIGHTS AND PRIVILEGES OF A PLANK OWNER

BE IT FURTHER UNDERSTOOD: That he is entitled also to a clear, free, open and unencumbered title to a single plank in the deck of the aforementioned illustrious unit. THIS FINAL, ACCURATE SELECTION WILL BE MADE IN ORDER OF SENIORITY according to the treasured, honorable records contained in Davey Jones' Log Book DISOBEY THESE ORDERS UNDER EXTREME PENALTY OF MY DISPLEASURE

Commissioned 4 April 75

Commanding

We all became "plank owners" when the navy officially recognized Project Quick Find in April 1975.

The Quick Find team. *From top left*: Dan Peterson, John Busch, Rick Hetzell, Gordon Sybrant, Jim Ruckman, Tom McHugh, and Michael Wood.

public street, where luckily it was late and there were not any cars. Down the street he went for a little fun, but then he turned around and drove back to the go-cart facility, back through the bushes, and returned the cart to the appropriate parking section. Luckily this young SEAL had a skilled chief watching over him, as he was able to talk the go-cart facility manager out of calling the police. Of course, there was some chief petty officer to junior second class petty officer calibration quickly to follow. Unfortunately, there are not any photos of this event.

Despite a few minor liberty incidents, under Chief Gordon Sybrant's leadership, Project Quick Find had become a successful project for the navy. The six trainers and the three working sea lions became a great team. We all became "plank owners" when the navy officially recognized Project Quick Find in April 1975.

6

CHANGE OF COMMAND

Like any military organization, change is inevitable, and a successful project and capability also leads to expansion of the capability. There is also the normal military change of duty requirements that result in personnel transfers. In this case, it was time for Gordy to transfer and be replaced by both an officer and a new chief. In came LT Dan Healey as our Project Quick Find OIC and Chief Pat Gruber as our senior enlisted leader. Personnel changes are a natural way of life in the military, and Project Quick Find was no exception.

During my time at Quick Find, the group commanders were CDR George Worthington and CDR Bill Early. Project OICs were LT Paul Plumb, LT Don Healy, LT Pete Molaris, and LT Don Ridgeway. Later, when I returned to Quick Find as a photojournalist, the OIC was LT Marshall Daugherty. There were only two chief petty officers during my time, and they were Chief Gordon Sybrant and Chief Patrick Gruber. Project Quick Find had many additional OICs, chiefs, and enlisted trainers who deserve credit for the continued success of the project.

There were other changes brewing at the same time after the navy officially recognized the marine mammal program. First to happen was officially changing the command name and organizational chain of command from Naval Inshore Warfare Command under EOD to Naval Inshore Undersea Warfare Group One under Naval Special Warfare (NSW). That led to a "Group" designation and the assignment of a full commander as the group commander. It also led to the assignment of a lieutenant as

These patches reflect the change of Project Quick Find's organizational chain of command from Naval Inshore Warfare Command (NIWC) to Naval Inshore Undersea Warfare Group One (IUWG-1).

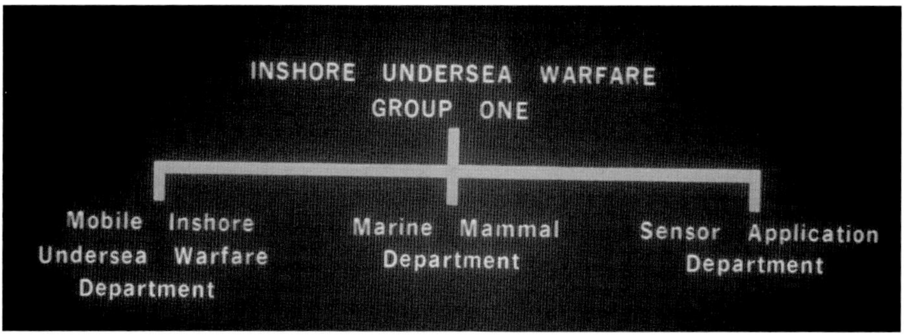

The Marine Mammal Department was a subdivision of IUWG-1.

OIC for both Project Quick Find and Project Short Time and with that, an increase in manning for trainers. This led to the first time introduction of East Coast SEALs as trainers.

Change came very swiftly with increased rules and regulations, professionalization of the trainers, introduction of doctrine, and processes. Some of this change was a little overwhelming for some, which eventually led to their departures. A good change that did occur quickly was our education process, in which we received formalized animal behavior courses and certification. It was good to finally learn the official terms for behavioral training that we learned on the job and had long been doing. We did discover that there was one practice that we did that was frowned upon and not approved and that was the practice of food deprivation as a form of incentive for the sea lions. We did withhold feeding them their five to ten pounds of smelt and mackerel on Sundays so that on Mondays they would be ready and willing to go to work. There seemed to never be any problems with the animals working on Mondays. We learned that food deprivation was *bad*. We did occasionally use other negative reinforcement or corporal punishment on sea lions that liked to bite and overtly tried to dominate situations. Sometimes we would use three fingers on an open palm to smack a biting sea lion on the snout. We also learned that corporal punishment was considered *bad*. Other than those two inappropriate behavioral training methods, we had been practicing very good methods, and now we knew what names to call those methods. The official animal behavior training was also timely because little did we know that soon we would be training naïve animals through new and more complex behaviors, and we were now skilled in the methodical process of operant conditioning.

A new major positive benefit that occurred with the change of command was the marine mammal program actually received a larger navy budget, and we were beginning to see facilities, equipment, and services that we

naval undersea center
marine mammal training course

presents this certificate to

PH2 M. P. Wood
INSHORUNSEAWARGRU ONE

for successful completion in a program of instruction in Marine Mammal Training Behavior & Systems 18 Sep - 8 Nov 1974

COMMANDER

had never seen before. Most of our acquisition process in the earlier days was the old process of cumshaw, or trading in civilian terms. We would trade a can of coffee or, better yet, a bag of abalone to the Sea Bees for any building materials and services that we required. We had a person, Jim Ruckman, skilled and assigned to that very duty of cumshaw. Now we actually had money and a budget. In fact, one of the first things that happened was a new marine mammal facility and pier were constructed on the opposite corner of NAB Coronado from our old and crumbling World War II Quonset hut building at Pier 13.

The new leadership and organizational structure did have a minor detrimental effect on our old Project Quick Find work relationships and evaluations. The original four of us second class petty officers all worked hard until the job was done every day and through some weekends, and our evaluations reflected that hard work equally. Under the new leadership, our equally hard work and dedication now had to be reflected in the new grading process of a "bell curve." How do you grade four equally hardworking and dedicated individuals on a bell curve? Our new chief petty officer had to explain to two of our guys why their normally

The navy's increased budget for the marine mammal program enabled the building of a new pier and floating facilities in San Diego Bay at the Naval Amphibious Base in Coronado.

straight across the board 3.8 to 4.0 (out of 4.0) grades had to be lowered because two guys had to have lower grades to reflect the bell curve. Luckily, I was not one of them, but a good friend of mine had his grades lowered to reflect the curve. It was fairly demoralizing to him and later played a small role in his decision to leave the navy. The new bureaucratic process had ramifications.

We knew there would be good and bad changes with the new organization and leadership. There were other changes that were neither good nor bad but just annoying. We now had to actually wear standard uniforms, resume strict grooming standards, report for muster, stand inspections, perform physical training, stand command watches, and worst of all, attend mandatory navy general training on subjects such as drug and alcohol abuse and sexual harassment, which met some resistance from the male-dominant organization. During this training, the female navy LT instructor made the mistake of asking this group of SEALs if they had any questions or comments. There was one outspoken redheaded, freckle-faced Puerto Rican first class petty officer with an Irish name who felt it was important to explain to the female LT that women were good for only one thing and that was "to keep them barefoot and pregnant." You could have heard a pin drop in that capacity-filled classroom. This female LT had experience working with SEALs and realized he said that to see how she would react to the shocking statement. She laughed it off but held her composure and command of the classroom. He was later heavily chastised by all the rest of us, not because we were sexual harassment sensitive, but because he unnecessarily prolonged our time and training in the sexual harassment class.

The sexual harassment training was also very timely because we soon received our first female prospective sea lion trainer. Just as we learned in our sexual harassment classes, she was afforded the same and equal sea lion indoctrination that all the previous male trainers received. She was introduced to harness training with Fatman. It seems Fatman is not sexist. He sunk his teeth deep into her unsuspecting thigh just like he did with all the other new male trainers. She decided right away after that incident that she did not want to train sea lions anymore. Initially, she was moved to the administrative office but soon after transferred to being a dolphin trainer in Project Short Time. She sure had a rude awakening in store in that project with the male dolphins during anti-swimmer training. Let's just say that swimming against the dolphins is a jolting experience once they come from out of nowhere in the dark, murky water and head butt you in your side or back. The male dolphins also had another natural biological urge, and even a big thick hawser line hanging in the water of a pen was not always enough to keep you safe. I don't remember whether she ever became a dolphin trainer or not. To be honest, it was not that she was female because there are many awesome female trainers both civilian and military. It was not her sex; it was her lack of willingness to deal with the natural animal behaviors.

The male trainer propensity for animal-like behavior and stupidity did not go totally unfounded. There was one brief moment in time during this transition period when two very experienced trainers exhibited a momentary lapse in judgment. LT Don Ridgeway, a former enlisted officer, was our new OIC, and he had a lot of respect and confidence in these two senior plank-owner trainers. He counted on them for help with running Quick Find because he and the chief were both new to marine mammals. Occasionally, we would need to transport sea lions to the NUC facility on Point Loma, which as the crow flies was just across the bay. Going by roads, the route took longer and went right through some old and seedy portions of San Diego. These trainers needed to transport Akahi to NUC for a routine medical checkup on the past heartworm issue. Normally, this transport task would require only one trainer to go, but the excuse was given that two trainers were needed to lift Akahi in his cage into and out of the truck bed. Technically that was a legitimate reason as far as weight and lift requirements were concerned, but there was an alternative reason for these two trainers to collaborate.

The trip there and the medical checkup on Akahi all went well and according to schedule. It was during the drive back through the seedy part of town that the plan deviated. There was a very popular adults-only bar called "Pacers—Just a Kiss Away" en route, and the truck "accidentally" pulled into the parking lot. It was early afternoon, so there were plenty of parking spots with some under the cool shade of a tree. "Why not?" they thought. "We will just have a couple of beers and then take Akahi back."

Pacer's topless bar lured a couple of trainers off their route when transporting Akahi back from a medical checkup.

Akahi wonders what all the hullabaloo is about, regarding the Pacer's stop.

Lieutenant Don Ridgeway reminded the wayward trainers of their priorities.

Even in the early afternoon, the topless bar had very attractive dancing ladies and that combined with a couple of beers seemed to cloud the two trainers' normally sound judgment.

Early afternoon turned into late afternoon, and suddenly the bartender handed the bar phone to one of the trainers saying that they had a call. A little surprised about who might be calling because no one knew they were there, they took the phone. It was LT Don Ridgeway. His prior enlisted experience and route analysis had helped him deduce where the two trainers might be since they were late in getting back to the command. It did not take a brain surgeon to find the phone number to Pacer's either. Luckily, it was a cool day, and Akahi was okay in the cage under the shade of a tree. The two trainers didn't do anything else real stupid like bringing Akahi into the bar to meet the ladies, though they probably could have gotten some extra attention for introducing a real sea lion. After the very brief phone call, the two trainers quickly paid the bar tab and drove safely back to the command for their awaiting chastisement and restricted duty assignments. The days of "zero tolerance" had not hit the military yet, but the thirty-day restriction was still "attention getting."

Times continued to change. The navy saw the success with Project Quick Find, and the dolphin Short Time program was demonstrating success. The navy also had a big mine warfare burdening requirement that could benefit from the marine mammals both in recovering training

Above: Change of command brought a new group of trainers and some additional sea lions. *From left to right*: Leading Petty Officer Tom McHugh with Fatman, me with Sinbad, Mike Kelly with Akahi, OIC Lieutenant Don Ridgeway, Jack Kennedy, Chief Petty Officer Pat Gruber, Rick Hetzell, Eddie Felton with Gump, Gary Young with Snitch, and John Jauzems with Scooner. Coronado Bay bridge in the background.

Right: Me getting love from Sinbad on the dressing stand.

mines after mine laying exercises but also in the detection, location, and marking of live enemy mines. Most enemy mines utilize some form of magnetic, seismic, or acoustic influence to initiate detonation. Most divers, diver propulsion vehicles, and submersibles all have a heavy magnetic signature, which require significant investment and training of low magnetic signature divers and equipment. Sea lions and dolphins have zero magnetic, seismic, or acoustic signatures and were prime candidates for mine detection, location, and marking requirements. Whether sea lions or dolphins would be the best choice for any of these mine warfare requirements would be determined only after training both of the marine mammals in the multiple behaviors required to detect, locate, or mark a mine.

7

SEALS CAPTURE SEA LIONS

Testing and demonstrating the best marine mammal course of action for the new mine warfare requirement would necessitate a much higher inventory of sea lions and dolphins. I do not know how or if any new dolphins were acquired. This new mine warfare requirement did lead to one of the most fun and exciting experiences of my time in the navy, and that was the capturing of sea lions at a rookery on San Nicholas Island (SNI).

We conducted two captures at selected rookeries on San Nicholas Island, California, with one occurring in January 1975 and one during February 1976 under close supervision and oversight from NUC veterinarians and in accordance with all marine mammal act requirements of the day. LT Dan Healy and NUC Vet Jay Sweeney led the first capture in 1975, and LT Don Ridgeway and NUC Vet Bob Gunnels led the second 1976 capture. We were based out of SNI quarters and used the island icehouse to house the captured sea lions in a cool and wet environment.

There were actually two separate captures in 1975 and 1976, but the elements and results were essentially the same. The main goal was to capture one-year-old males as determined by the scientific and marine mammal leadership that males would be the best choice. I do not know whether top-down guidance was provided on what specific rookeries we were to use, but we did seem to scout out a couple rookeries during a pre-capture reconnaissance.

Top: Quick Find crew prepares to load sea lions and equipment onto the cargo flight from San Nicholas Island to North Island Naval Air Station in Coronado.

Middle left: OIC LT Dan Healy and vet Jay Sweeney meet with the sea lion capture crew in front of the San Nicholas barracks for the first sea lion capture in 1975.

Middle right: OIC LT Don Ridgeway (*far left*) confers with NUC vet Bob Gunnels (*far right*) on a cliff overlooking a sea lion rookery, preparing a plan for the second capture in 1976.

Left: NUC vets Jay Sweeney and Bob Gunnels discuss the capture plan on a cliff overlooking the sea lion rookery st San Nicholas Island.

The rookeries consisted of a mixture of California sea lions (*Zalophus californianus*) and elephant seals (*Mirounga*). The main difference between sea lions and seals is that sea lions have visible external ears. More obvious was that elephant seals were three to four times the size of the sea lions. The rookeries ranged in size and typography, with most of them on sandy beaches and a few of them on rocky bluffs. This difference in rookery locations significantly altered the capture approach, method, and concealment. We definitely had to be able to approach the herds from a seaward location so when they alerted and began their escape toward the safety and sanctuary of the water, they would actually have to run right by us to get to the water. This capture approach did rule out conducting any captures on the rocky bluffs. The beach captures caused us to have to come out of concealment sooner than we would have liked. We decided to cross the rocky shorelines and risk the longer out-in-the-open approach because it would cause less stress and eliminate or reduce injury to all the sea lions and seals in the rookery due to the sandy bottom.

Most of us had never been on a sea lion capture except for some of the NUC personnel. Also, our capture tools and implements seemed to be rudimentary to include hoop nets, larger area nets, blocking boards, capture by hand, and cages.

A view of the rookery on San Nicholas Island that was selected for the capture. A group of elephant seals rest in the higher section of the beach and the California sea lions gather on the lower part of the beach, closer to the water.

Captors use the rocky ledges adjacent to the rookery to hide their approach to the sea lions on the beach.

Captors stoop low for the final approach to the sea lion rookery to start the capture.

Left: Dan Peterson carries a large capture net down to the beach.

Right: Jack Kennedy holds down the hind flippers of a newly captured sea lion, waiting for the NUC personnel to check the sex of the animal.

The NUC personnel showed us how to use the hoop nets on selected animals, how to capture a sea lion just by grabbing its hind flippers, using the larger area net to capture several animals, and finally how to use the blocking boards to isolate and herd an animal. All of these methods minimized the chance of physical injury to the sea lions but in some cases did cause injury to the captors. Captor injury was not of concern.

In both capture cases, the pre-capture reconnaissance caused us to choose a beach rookery that was close to the rocky bluffs. This enabled us to sneak along the rocky ledges out of sight until we got to the bluff edge next to the rookery on the sand. Then we would climb down the rocky ledges and get into the knee- to ankle-deep water and leave the concealment of the bluffs. In most cases, the rookeries did not alert until we came out into the open along the beach.

There was one case when captors were hunched over using the rocks and ledges to conceal their approach. One of the captors in the lead placed his hand down on what he thought was a rock, but it turned out to be a sleeping bull elephant seal that woke up with a start, rising

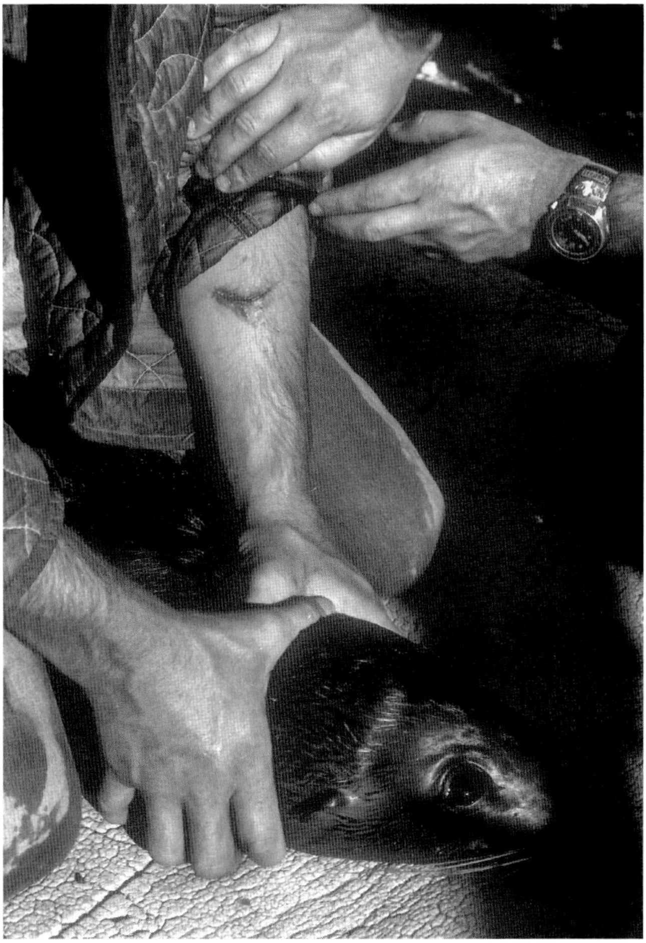

Left: Jack Kennedy holds down a sea lion and the NUC vet inspects the sea lion bite wound on Jack's arm.

Below: Captors lie down, keeping a low profile as they survey the rookery below.

to full height and bellowing out an alert that echoed across the cliffs, beach berms, and sandy beach. This caused the entire rookery to begin scurrying for the water and the captors to race for the water line to cut off the animals' approach to the ocean. On most of the approaches, we began slowly from the water's edge toward the sandy beaches and dunes,

Above, left: Captors weave their way through the rocky shoreline as some of the bull sea lions escape to the water.

Above, right: Captors crawl in low profile along a sand berm into the open beach area where the sea lions are becoming alert.

A rookery of California sea lions alerts to the presence of the captors and begins running to the safety of the water.

Left: NUC corpsman and lumberjack-sized Rob Horseman weaves his way through the elephant seals to reach the sea lions.

Right: Dan Peterson (*left*) and Rob Horseman (*right*) carry their hoop nets and run up the beach to select and capture a yearling sea lion.

and that is generally when the majority of the sea lions and some of the elephant seals would alert and begin their running, waddling, and undulating toward and past us and into the safety of the water. Not all of the elephant seals would alert or run. It seemed that some of the larger elephant seals would still lie on the beach, never move, and barely look up at us as if in disdain of our puny presence. I guess our puny presence was not much of a threat.

The goal was to capture male yearlings that ranged in weight from thirty to fifty pounds. Obviously, we could not tell the sex of the animals until we captured them. So as we approached the herd from the water line, we would pick out yearlings farther up the beach and focus on a single animal instead of getting distracted by all the animals running by. Once the approach from the water line to the beach began, it all seemed to become a cacophony of loud noise, splashing, movement, and even a thunderous roar and vibration. A few captors would take a splashy wet fall as they missed their target animal with the hoop net or hand capture. It is true, the bigger they are, the harder they fall. Not many tried to use the blocking boards or the larger nets during the initial rush, when the animals passed by us; the overall activity seemed to slow a little, but the loud noise escalated as the animals out in the safety of the water were still directing their loud barking toward those still on the beach. The dunes and rocky cliffs also added to the echo of the boisterous barking from the sea so the noise continued. A couple of captors even managed to capture two sea lions at a time.

Above, left: Rob Horseman and Bob Gunnels lift up the hind flippers of the sea lion to check the sex.

Above, right: John Jauzems reconfigures the large capture net to give the captured sea lions more room to move.

Left, top: LT Don Ridgeway (*left*) holds the hind flippers of a sea lion while others check the sex of the captured sea lions.

Left, bottom: Captors use a large net to herd and capture several sea lions.

Sea lions escape to the safety of the water and surf zone and continue loudly barking warnings to the rest of the rookery on the beach.

Dan Peterson (*left*) holds a sea lion in a hoop net while Rick Hetzell (*right*) holds onto two sea lions in hoop nets.

Some of the captors caught their animals during the initial rush, with most using a hoop net and a few capturing by hand. Half of the captors participated in the capture process.

The other half of the captors started herding and isolating both individual and small groups of yearlings and capturing them with the larger nets or hand capture. There were a few that did not capture because they were needed to help the vets go around to determine the sex of the captured animals. If they were females, they were immediately released. The vets continued inspecting the animals, ensuring they were the desired age, and if too young or old, they were released regardless of sex. As things began to quiet down, the vets looked even closer to see if there were any outward appearances of injury, illness, or sickness, and those would also be let go. Each captor then tried to calm down each animal, and spare personnel began to bring the portable cages down to the beach. We loaded two animals into each cage and then carried the cages into the shallow water for a little while to help cool and calm the animals.

Then came the long process of walking back up the beach, where four personnel would carry each cage of two animals through the soft sand, up the beach berm, and up the even steeper dirt- and crevice-riddled road to the top of the cliff or bluff where the trucks were parked. The roads were in too poor of condition to drive the trucks to the beach. We brought big water spray cans with us to keep spraying and wetting down the animals to keep them cool during the climb and while in the trucks. Once the animals were safely secured, we did finally stop for our own wet down, water, and meal break.

Once we had the trucks loaded with personnel, sea lions, and equipment, we began the very slow and bumpy drive up the rest of the hill to the one and only road that circled the island. The drive on this road was fairly smooth and short to the island cement and block icehouse with running water.

The captors took a short break at the SNI icehouse and then began to open the "barbershop" and the "Frankenstein lab." Assigned captors then began to select, isolate, and hold down each sea lion to shave a small patch of tail fur to draw blood. Each blood sample was labeled and put in a slow shaking device to prevent the blood samples from coagulating. The vets then broke out their microscopes and glass slides to test and inspect each sample.

I do not know what tests the vets were conducting or what their parameters were, but some of the animals were put back in cages and released back into the rookeries. The young male yearlings that were left had

Opposite, top: Four captors carry a portable cage with two sea lions to the water to help cool them down.

Opposite, middle: Captors congregate around the sea lions in the cages at the water line. This helped cool down the animals before the long hike up the road to the trucks at the top of the berm.

Opposite, bottom: Captors carry the sea lions in the cages to the trucks on the hilltop.

This page, top: Captors have loaded caged animals onto the truck and stop for a water break.

This page, bottom: Personnel make sure the sea lion cages are secure in the trucks and begin the laborious process of driving up the rugged road to the island roadway above.

Top: Captors drive the trucks on the only roadway on the island back to the icehouse.

Bottom: Trucks pull up to the icehouse ready to unload the sea lions.

passed the sex and medical exams. During this testing process, there was one young sea lion that stood out among the group. Every time the guys would go into the icehouse to select another sea lion for testing, this one animal kept sneaking out the open door and escaping. He did this time after time to the point that we gave him the name Papillion after the famed French prisoner who kept escaping prisons.

I took a liking to Papillion's strong spirit and decided to select him as my animal to train when we got them back to San Diego. Some of the animals went to NUC, some went to Sea World, but most would go to Project Quick Find and join the naïve animal training program for basic training

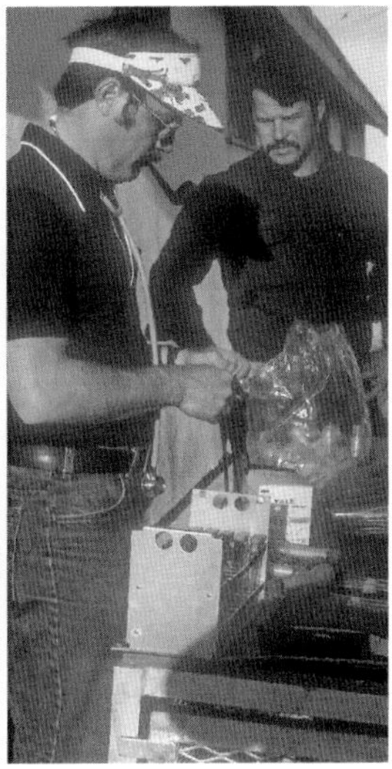

Above, left: Rob Horseman and Dan Peterson carry a sea lion out for medical exam and blood sampling.

Above, middle: Captors draw blood from the sea lion.

Above, right: NUC vet Bob Gunnels and LT Don Ridgeway review the blood samples.

Left: Young captured sea lion Papillion makes a break for it in the open doorway to escape but is corralled by a captor.

Captured sea lions huddle together under the dripping water in the icehouse.

behaviors and then later for the mine search and marking program the navy was starting.

The group of young sea lions got a one-day rest and recuperation period in the icehouse before the airline flight to San Diego. During that overnight rest period, we checked on the sea lions continuously, and some of us even stayed in the icehouse overnight to look out after them. We would sit on some empty plastic milk containers resting against the wall with our legs stretched out. A strange thing began to happen the longer we sat there. First it was Papillion. He waddled over and began to sniff my legs and then climbed up my legs until his torso was high up resting on my chest and he was looking directly into my eyes. I was a little nervous at first because although he was a yearling, his canines were right next to my throat. To my surprise, Papillion rested his head on my shoulders and went to sleep. I felt like a daddy with a newborn. Some of the other sea lions then did the same thing with the two other captors, Rob Horseman and LT Don Ridgeway. Three sea lions lay down next to Horseman's six-foot-plus prone body on the floor, and one sea lion climbed on Ridgeway's lap and went to sleep. We were under no illusions that these animals liked us; they were just looking for a warm place to sleep. It was still one of the coolest experiences ever.

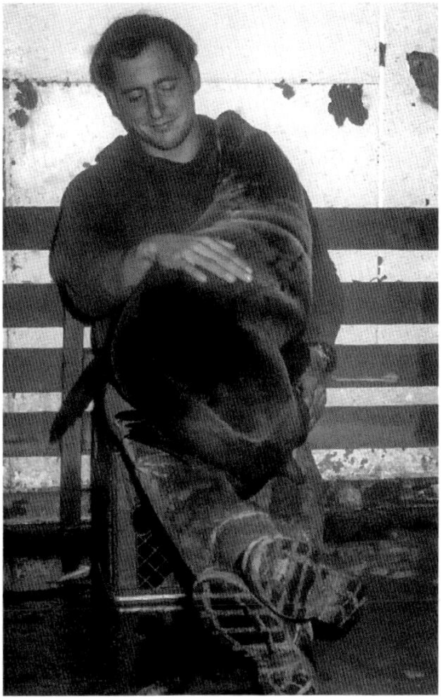

Left: Papillion crawls up on my legs and rests his head on my chest to get warm from the cold icehouse floor.

Right: A sea lion crawls up on the lap of LT Don Ridgeway to rest and get warm.

Six-foot-plus Rob Horseman lies down on a pallet and two sea lions crawl onto his body for warmth.

Top: A truck loaded with sea lions and equipment waiting at the Naval Outlying Field, San Nicholas Island.

Bottom: Airfield crew pushes the pallet load of sea lion cages onto the cargo aircraft.

The next day, a couple more animals were released back to the rookery, and then we loaded up all the animals, equipment, and personnel and waited at the San Nicholas Island air terminal for our flight back to Naval Air Station Coronado.

Depending on which capture it was, the flight conditions would vary from either a Navy C-9 jet to a commercial prop cargo plane. When on a

Top, left: Aircraft crewman secures Project Quick Find equipment and sea lion cages onboard the aircraft for the flight home to Coronado.

Top, right: Civilian and military passengers hover around the captured sea lions in their cages onboard the commercial aircraft.

Bottom, left: Papillion takes his first steps into his new home at the newly built floating sea lion pen.

Bottom, right: Papillion looks out of the fencing as he sits in the tub of water in his pen, where he will be temporarily quarantined from the other sea lions.

passenger C9, we could not escape the requirement to show off the sea lions and discuss the capture on San Nicholas Island.

The passengers also would get an occasional rude awakening when one of the grey plastic-cage inserts would leak and the sea lion excrement would flow the full length of the aircraft passageway. The sea lions were not concerned, or impressed, with the passengers' GS-position or military rank.

Once we arrived home, we introduced the sea lions to their new home, where food was plentiful and the work light.

8

MISSION EXPANSION

A lot of things changed about this time, including personnel, sea lions, and missions. Three Quick Find plank owners were still around, including Hetzell, Peterson, and me, but we also received several SEALs from the East Coast teams, including Gary Young, Mike Kelley, John Jauzems, Chuck McPhearson, Jack Kennedy, and three new West Coast guys, Bud Dennehy, Tom Waples, and Eddie Felton. Some sea lion changes occurred, including new sea lions such as Sinbad the volunteer, Scooner, and Papillion, with Gump being transferred to Sea World. Scooner and Papillion were caught at SNI.

Plank owners had the duties of training up the new sea lion trainers for the traditional ASROC recovery missions while simultaneously improvising methods, procedures, and equipment to begin training the new naïve sea lions, as well as coming up with ways to train the animals for a mine search and recovery mission.

Peterson, Hetzell, and I started with the training of the newly captured sea lions and putting them through the operant conditioning basics. We were not given much guidance or funds for developing the new mine mission, such as guidance on the expected type of mines to search and recover or the prototype equipment such as mine-like shapes, grabber devices, or even devices the sea lions could use to carry the new grabber devices. There was a bit of a timing misfortune. There were no more EOD personnel attached to Quick Find. Both Sybrant and Busch had transferred. It was EOD that currently performed the practice mine recovery missions for the navy, and

All new trainers learned to train experienced sea lions in ASROC recovery in San Diego Bay. Here, Gary Young is the coxswain, Tom Waples handling line, and Chuck McPhearson training the sea lion, Thor, with a D5 training grabber.

we sure could have used their expertise both as EOD technicians and as experienced sea lion trainers.

Peterson, Hetzell, and I all worked with the naïve sea lions about this time in varying capacities, and one of our first duties was to locate potential mine-like shapes. We made many trips to the military defense reutilization and marketing office (DRMO) establishments, commonly called "dumps" in the civilian world. We eventually located several mine-like targets, some of which included real but inert mines, but they ended up being way too heavy for training purposes. We eventually settled on a long but very light aluminum rocket pod shape that was "mine-like." This was a shape that one man could handle launching and recovering from a small boat.

One of the best ways to learn more about the mine search and recovery mission was to participate in an actual EOD mine exercise (MINEX) of finding, marking, and recovering mines dropped from an aircraft. I was fortunate to be able to participate in the MINEX at San Clemente Island (SCI) with an EOD team. The first thing I learned was that a MINEX involved aircraft airdropping mines in a designated area off SCI, but instead of just one or two items like a QAST shot, they dropped as many as thirty

We used aluminum rocket pods that had a mine-like shape to train the sea lions.

Here the chosen mine-shape is floated on the surface to start the basic mine training behaviors. John Jauzems is driving, Rick Hetzell is line handling, and Ed Felton is the trainer during this training session in Glorietta Bay right next to our facility at Pier 13.

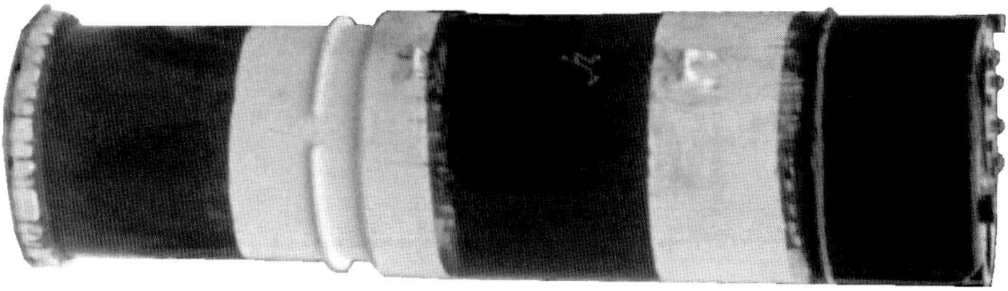

Above: This is an EOD exercise mine and was a candidate QF mock-mine.

Below: The practice mines were dropped from an aircraft rather than shot off a boat.

mines. The interesting part was the airdrops may or may not occur where they were supposed to drop.

The airdrop accuracy of the mines meant that we spent a lot of time in the zodiac rubber boats hanging over the gunwales, listening on the pinger receiver headsets, and trying to locate each of the mines' attached 37 kHz pinger. The problem was twofold: the range of detecting a mine was greater, and there was potential confusion of multiple mine pinger signatures in the same water area at the same time, which made directing the boat driver to the right location a little problematic. Slowly, over a three-day period, we began to isolate the mine pinger signatures, and as we came as close to the mine as we could with the pinger, we had to dive over the side, swim down, and try to visually or acoustically locate and mark the mine underwater. Most of the time, the surface pinger location was accurate, and we were able to find the mines and mark them with buoys. Then the LCU (landing craft utility) would come by and recover and crane each mine onto the boat.

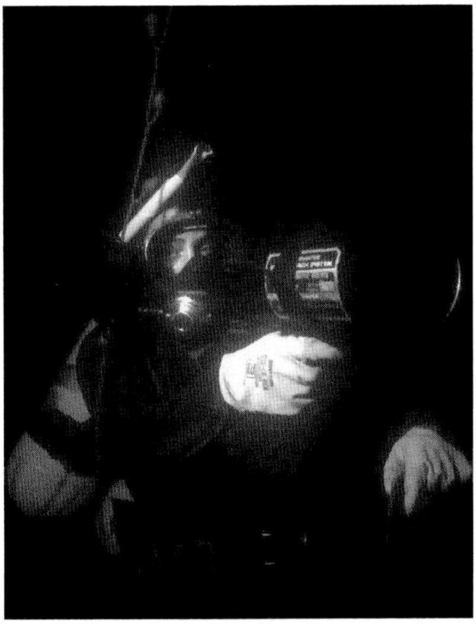

Right: I use a pinger reveiver underwater to lovate a practice mine in ninety feet of water off San Clemente Island during an EOD mine recovery exercise.

Below: The airdrop's poor accuracy made it much harder to pinpoint the location of the mine with the pinger signatures. We had to dive down to visually or acoustically locate the mine underwater.

The work meant twelve to fourteen hours a day in a wetsuit listening on a headset and then responding quickly with dive gear to locate and mark each mine for recovery. It took every minute of our three-day mission to locate and recover all of the thirty practice mines. It was a very long, hardworking, wet, and windy time, but it was an incredible learning experience. Upon completion, I definitely learned what it was going to take for a sea lion to locate and mark a mine-like shape.

One of the problems with this new requirement for training naïve animals and training for a new mission was that all the old Quick Find assets and equipment were still required for the traditional ASROC recovery mission. This meant we did not have the work barge, winch and crane, support boats, mock-up targets, or grabber devices as available as we would like, especially the use of the work barge. This called for us to improvise like the old days in Quick Find. Our first mission was to replace the barge to get the animals to the maritime training area. There was a sixteen-foot Boston Whaler that had been resting upside down on our equipment barge unused. It needed significant hull fiberglass repair work and a refurbished outboard motor. I had the skill to repair and paint the fiberglass on the hull, so that part was easy. Our organization now had available an outboard motor mechanic and repair shop that refurbished and installed the seventy-horsepower Johnson engine. Now, I just had to figure out a way to carry four sea lion cages and the mock-up targets on the refurbished sixteen-foot Boston Whaler. That solution came in an inspiration when I built a six- by ten-foot plywood deck across the seating in the whaler where the sea lion cages could be bolted to the removable plywood decking. I will admit that loading the four cages with sea lions and equipment did make the whaler a little top-heavy, but this system was not meant for going out to sea. It was for inside the harbor training only, and it proved quite effective and safe. There would not always be four cages with animals on board. That was just the maximum capacity the whaler could hold. Usually there would only be two animals and cages on board the boat.

The marine transportation problem was solved. I just needed to figure out what type of mines would be used and what mock-ups we would need to fabricate to serve as training targets. The problem was it was still not known whether the mine targets would be traditional round contact mines or if they would be influence mines, which took many shapes but most would be two- to three-foot-diameter cylindrical shapes. That said, there were also conical shape influence mines like the Manta mine, but it was not predominant in other countries' mine inventories.

I decided to go with the cylindrical shape because that would represent the preponderance of U.S. and foreign influence mines. Then I had to decide what to use as a mock-up mine trainer. U.S. inventory of training mines would be the logical choice, but a large craft with a winch and crane was required to put these mine trainers in and out of the water. All I had was a sixteen-foot whaler with a human-powered lift, so the mine trainers were out of the question. An inspiration occurred: go to DRMO (military junkyard) to

Trainers Mike Kelley (*left*) and Gary Young (*right*) use the sixteen-foot Whaler, converted to cary sea lions and the cages.

see what shapes were available to represent a two- or three-foot-diameter by five- to six-foot-long cylindrical shape. Numerous shapes were available, and I acquired them, but the one that seemed to work out the best was a former helicopter 2.75-inch Zuni-rocket pod. All that was needed was to remove the rocket holders inside the cylindrical shape pod, and a mock-up target of approximate shape, length, diameter, and, most importantly, lightweight aluminum was the final choice. We copied the ASROC paint scheme using mostly white color with black stripes in the middle of the mine-like shape to use as the appropriate sea lion target zone.

The grabber device was hand-cut aluminum-shaped and much larger than the mock-mine shape because the training grabber needed to be the diameter of a real mine. The existing D8 and D9 grabber devices were not large enough to encompass a mine shape sitting on the bottom of the ocean. Instead of reinventing the wheel, I did determine to use the grabber-type system for initial mine training, although I seriously doubted that the old type of grabber system could be effective and used to power through the sandy bottom to encompass the mine with a cable recovery system. What I did was build curved-shaped aluminum grabber arms that were representative of a three-foot-diameter cylindrical shape. There would not be an actual grabber mechanism, just a curved aluminum-shaped arm. Because this new, larger design was three times bigger than the current D8/D9 grabbers, I had to set the mine grabber up to be carried by either a nose cone or bite- plate system for the sea lion. Of course, that would mean training the sea lions to carry

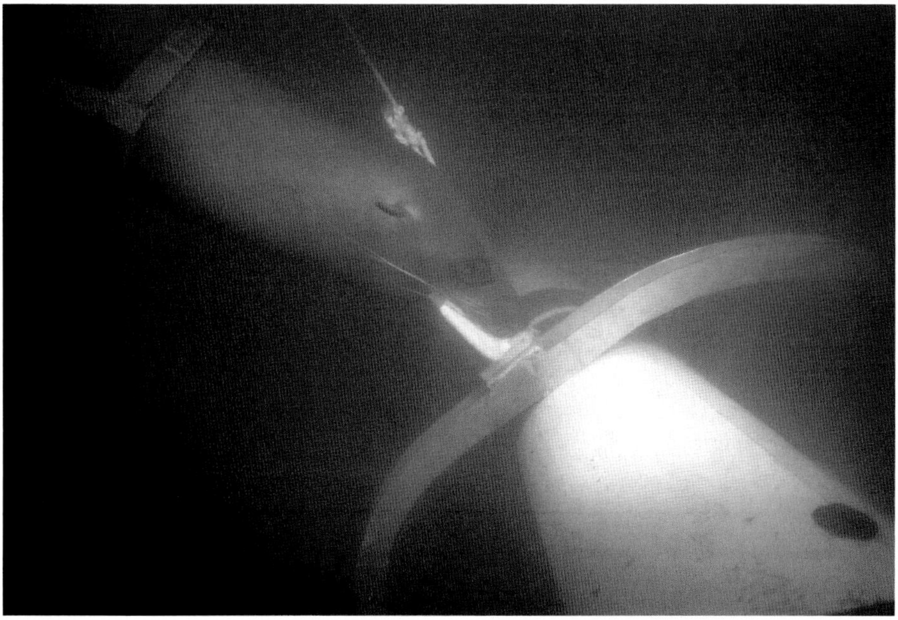

Sea lion Sinbad uses a bite plate to carry a prototype mine-marking device in the shallow and turbid waters near their home at Pier 13 to mark a practice mine target on the bottom.

either a nose cone or bite-plate system. I kept many of the other mine-like shapes I got from DRMO available in case this rocket pod mine mock-up did not work. Now the mine training could begin.

Peterson and Hetzell were putting the newly captured sea lions through their basic operant conditioning training. The sea lions had to be trained in the basic behavior of listening for the 9 kHz pinger and touching the pinger to indicate hearing the tone. A magnetic grabber attached to a nose cone trained the sea lion to wear the nose cone and accept the weight of the magnetic attachment device. Accepting a nose cone or a bite plate is basic behavior the naïve sea lion needed to learn. Peterson used a whistle as a bridge between good behavior and fish reward for the sea lion "getting dressed" in the harness. He rewarded the sea lion as he completed tightening the belly strap on the harness.

Once basic operant conditioning steps were completed, one of the next most important behaviors for the sea lion to learn was how to work from a small rubber boat. There were many steps in this process, from just walking the animal into the boat, riding on the gunwale, and diving from and returning to the boat both tethered and untethered. The photo on page 105

Right: Rick Hetzell hangs a 9 kHz pinger over the side of the work barge.

Below, left: Hetzell helps adjust the nose cup device to the sea lion wearing the muzzle, which provides protection from abrasion of the nose cone. *Below, right*: The sea lion gets a fish reward.

Bottom: Dan Peterson trains the sea lion to accept the weight of the nose cone by using a magnetic attachment device.

In this photo, I am driving the boat, Busch is line handler, and Hetzell is the trainer.

shows Rick Hetzell training his naïve sea lion through all of these steps and his sea lion, Scooner, jumping out of the water and onto the gunwale of the rubber boat. Hetzell's reaction is instinctive as the sea lion brings a good amount of water with him as he jumps into the boat. The wetsuit muzzle on the animal's mouth is to protect the animal from abrasion by the grabber device cup and has no impact on the animal's ability to breathe, eat, or bite. The muzzle easily opens as his mouth opens.

My first sea lion that I had full responsibility for was Sinbad, a volunteer into the Quick Find project. I used Sinbad, who already completed this basic training, as the early mine training sea lion. In the meantime, I did begin basic operant conditioning with Papillion.

Sinbad's story is an interesting one. Sea lions would much rather do a couple hours of work a day for the five to ten pounds of fish than have to hunt for their food all night and day. I don't know if there is a marine mammal telegraph system in the water, but word must have gotten out about this easier sea lion lifestyle of working a couple hours and then lying around all day in the sun with full stomachs. Sinbad must have heard the marine mammal

Sometimes a sea lion did not get his fish reward if he did not complete the task correctly. Here, Rick's sea lion does not seem happy about not receiving a reward.

I use fish to entice Sinbad onto the thirty-six-foot work barge in San Diego Bay. This is Sinbad before he was enlisted for Project Quick Find duty.

word. We would go out to sea every day about two to three miles off the coast of Point Loma to train the animals for ASROC recovery. Suddenly, we started seeing this young sea lion popping his head up next to the barge at sea. He was a little different because he would just hang around and watch. Other sea lions would make a quick check of the barge and sea lions and then take off. Even more amazing was we started throwing smelt to Sinbad, and he ate the dead fish. Typically, you would have to train the sea lions to eat dead fish. We figured we would not see him again. The next day at sea, he showed up again and came even closer to the barge. We threw him some fish, and again he ate. This time we put some fish on the deck of the barge just out of his reach in the water. Sure enough, Sinbad jumped up onto the barge deck and ate the fish. Okay, okay, this is too weird. We left and came back the next day, and again Sinbad showed up without prompting. He just jumped onto the deck. This time we left a trail of fish that led right into one of our barge deck cages, and Sinbad followed the fish trail all the way into the cage. We closed the cage, and he did not freak out. I opened the cage right away and gave him a few fish in the water to get him off the boat. We were not sure if we were breaking any marine mammal rules at the time. This was the early '70s, so the rules were not as strict then. We went back to the base and figured that would be the last we would see of Sinbad because it was Friday; the weekend was coming, and we would not be back out to sea until the following Monday. To our surprise, he showed back up like he was ready to go to work, jumping back on the barge. We led him into the cage, fed him some fish, and let him stay in there while we trained the other animals. He rode back with us on the barge, and when we got to the base, we released him into San Diego Bay. The next day, he showed up to the barge while still tied up to our base pier before going to sea. This animal was persistent about becoming a Quick Find volunteer. We did not take him that day because we needed to check with NUC about whether to let him volunteer. I am not sure at what level we got approval, but the word I got was to go ahead and take him in but to make sure he went to NUC for a full physical. That is how Sinbad became the first volunteer to the Quick Find project.

Now that we had necessary transportation, mock-up targets, and grabber devices ready and available, it was time to begin developing the mine search and marking behaviors. Sinbad was the first animal to start this training since he already had learned the basic behaviors of harness training, 9 kHz pinger listening and touching, nose cone/grabber, diving tethered, and identifying and marking an ASROC mock-up. Papillion was in the process of completing that same training.

Left: I reward Sinbad with fish for a good training dive at sea.

Right: Tom Waples uses fish to entice Sinbad onboard the work barge.

Rick Hetzell train Thor in naïve animal behaviors, including dressing stand mounting and harness training on the work barge as it is tied up next to the floating pen.

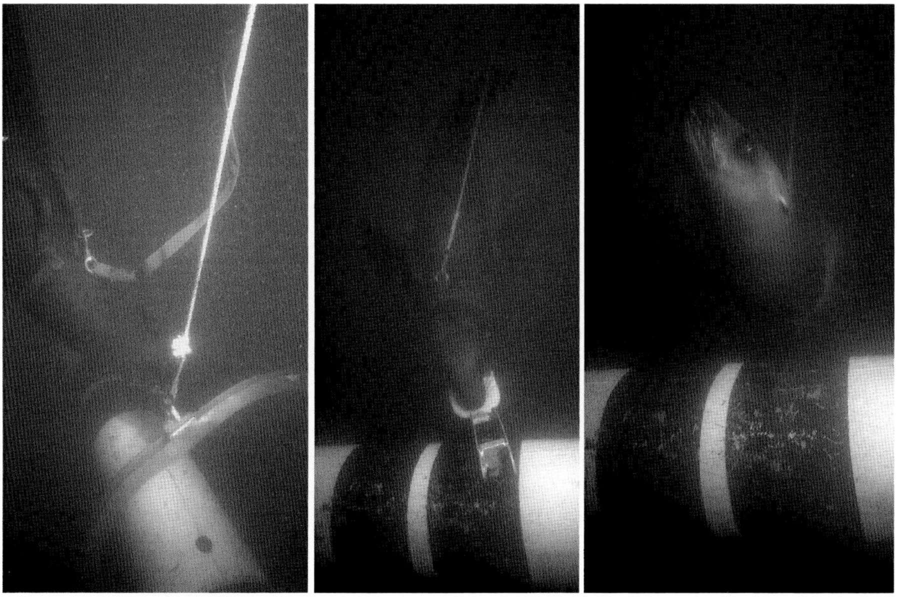

This sequence of events shows Sinbad with a bite plate and mine grabber hitting the wrong part of the mine (*left photo*). Then he hits the correct spot at the middle of the mine (*middle photo*). Sinbad checks his work and swims back to the surface (*right photo*).

The first behavior was to train the animals where to place a grabber on the mock-up mine, which was all white with dual black stripes about twelve inches thick, each in the center of the cylinder. This behavior introduction began with placing the mine-shape on the deck in the pen and just letting Sinbad touch particular parts of the mine shape. When he touched the black stripes in the middle, we would blow the whistle and then reward him with a fish. Sinbad learned very quickly where to touch his nose on the mine shape. Then we hung the mine shape in the pen community pool just at the water surface and had Sinbad swim from one side of the pool to the other and touch the black stripes. Then we introduced the 9 kHz pinger sound to the mine shape. We built an aluminum mine grabber shape and attached it to a nose cone and had Sinbad place the grabber device on the middle of the mine shape. The mock grabber was about three times the size of the D8 and D9 grabbers, and it seemed very cumbersome for Sinbad to hold this grabber with a nose cone. So we had to train him how to use a bite-plate system, which he picked up very quickly. The bite plate was connected to the mine grabber, and Sinbad was able to control the grabber device much easier when swimming, so we switched over to

Sinbad looks around impatiently, waiting for me to give him the signal to dive in the water during a training session at sea off Point Loma.

Carrying my five-gallon bucket of fish, I walk Sinbad from the work barge to the Z-boat.

that system. Papillion had just graduated from his marine mammal basic training, so we started working with him on the basic mine behaviors, as well.

Once Sinbad and Papillion graduated from the basic mine behaviors, we started placing the mine shape with pinger in about ten feet of water right in our pier area. This became more of a challenge for the two because the pier-area waters are murky in that part of San Diego Bay, and the visibility was about two to five feet. This required the sea lions to rely on their audio skills to listen for the 9 kHz pinger until the mine shape came into view. This part of the training process took much longer because both Sinbad and Papillion had very little practical experience listening and locating the pinger, especially in murky water. One of the problems with placing a target in shallow, murky water that required more of the sea lion's audio skills was that the pinger noise would sometimes reverberate, making it echo and more difficult for the sea lion to obtain the proper direction. It would be almost like an echo underwater but from several directions. We decided to transport to deeper bay waters, between twenty to thirty feet deep, to conduct the training. Not only would the water visibility clear up a bit, but also it would eliminate the pinger echo, making it easier for the animal to get a bearing to the pinger. There was a risk involved with this decision. The animals had not yet mastered the location of the mine in ten feet of water and now we were making them go ten to twenty feet. It was a calculated risk, but it seemed worth it.

This now meant that both animals would need to be trained to board the sixteen-foot Boston Whaler, enter the whaler cages, and tolerate a bumpier ride than what they were used to on the thirty-six-foot work barge. The whaler towed the Z-bird behind to use as a workboat and served as the support platform. We decided to train in the waters next to the NUC piers, which was about a thirty-minute boat transit for the animals. The water visibility there was a good ten feet, if not better, and the water depth was between twenty and thirty feet, depending on where we placed the mine target. This is where we conducted the majority of the mine search and marking training. The clearer and deeper waters did help the sea lions to locate the pinger noise, and it gave them greater visibility range to see the target and maneuver to the correct position on the mine shape. The training continued here for a few months until we were confident the animals were consistently locating and marking the mine shape in at least thirty feet of water and that they were weaned off the attached tether line. Removing the tether line is always a nervous time because the animal is able to take off if desired. Hopefully, the previous tether line conditioning would make them think they couldn't swim away. Removing the tether line also simplified rubber boat operations because there was only need for tending one reel of line instead of the two: one reel for the animal and one reel for the grabber device.

The next step was to take the sea lions into gradually deeper water. This was problematic because the sixteen-foot whaler was not made for going out to sea. Now we needed to coordinate schedules for use of the thirty-six-foot work barge so we could take the sea lions first out to the Zuniga Point area, which was just at the end of the San Diego Bay rock jetty where we could still have calmer waters but achieve at least sixty feet of water depth. It was around this time that we had our first catastrophe when Sinbad died. I do not remember what was the cause of death, but I do know it was not heartworms. I had become very attached to Sinbad but had to overcome that and continue the training with Papillion, who fortunately was progressing very well. My memory is a little shaky here, but I believe we were also getting Scooner trained in the mine project at this time, so we still had two mine project sea lions. The next minor catastrophe occurred due to a momentary lapse in human judgment. All this time we were emplacing the mine shape into various depths of water, I would always free dive to the bottom to make sure the target was placed correctly on the bottom. It could really confuse

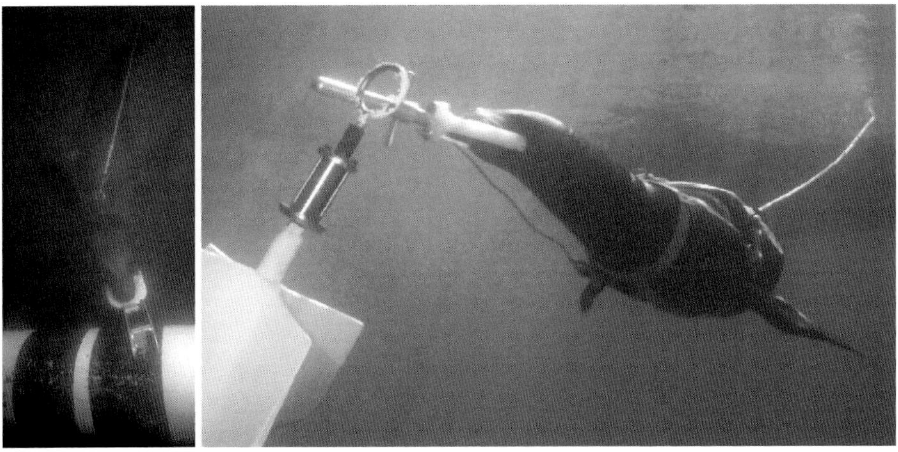

Left: The tether line is connected to the sea lion's body harness, and there is another tether line connected to the grabber device, requiring a total of two tether lines. *Right*: There is only one tether line that is connected to the grabber. The sea lion is free of any tether line.

the animals if the target landed vertically instead of horizontally on the bottom and could invalidate a whole day of training.

Up until this time, my free diving to check the target was easy in the ten to thirty feet of water, regardless of visibility, because I just followed the anchor line down. Now that we were training at Zuniga Point, where the water was colder and deeper, it meant putting on a wetsuit and donning full dive gear to go to the bottom and check the target. The first couple of times I used dive gear and a wetsuit to check the target. Then I ditched the gear but kept the wetsuit and free dived sixty feet down to check the target. Free diving worked okay to sixty feet. It was a little tiring and strenuous, but luckily all I had to do was check the target and not move it, then surface. My previous experience of spear fishing and free diving came in handy. Then a "brain fart" occurred to me. Why not ditch the wetsuit and ride an anchor down to the bottom to conserve air and energy to check the target? The second brilliant idea came to me to do this new target checking method when our QF officer-in-charge (OIC) came out to sea with us for the first time to check on the status of the mine training. I was confident in my lung and free-diving capacity, so why not do it when the OIC was there? Nothing would be different. We drove the barge to the Zuniga Point training area and dropped the weighted mine target over the side. The wind and sea conditions were calm, so it was easy for the barge to maintain station over the target. Then one of the guys lowered the barge's thirty-five-pound Danforth anchor over the bow of the barge and held it there until I entered the water with my fins and facemask. The task was simple: ride the anchor down to sixty feet, conserve air and energy, check out the target, and swim back to the surface. Easy! Once I was ready and gripping the anchor line, they released the anchor, and down I went, clearing my ears quickly as I descended. No problems so far. The anchor hit the bottom near the target, but suddenly there was an overwhelming cold feeling in my chest, and it seemed like someone had taken a vacuum cleaner and sucked all the air out of my lungs. Suddenly, on the bottom, I realized I had zero air left in my lungs and I was craving air. Luckily, I was able to remain calm and swim back up the anchor line as my chest began to convulse for more air. There was a slight relief as I neared the surface, but I seemed to get dizzy. I reached the surface and began a loud gasp for air, and everyone on board knew there was a problem. They also saw that I was bleeding from my nose. They helped me out of the water, and my main consuming thought was how I had so brilliantly impressed the OIC with my performance. *Not!* They did a quick neurological check, which I cleared, but the nose bleed and coldness in my chest were major concerns. They loaded me into the support boat and drove me to the recompression chamber at Point Loma for a diving medical officer check. Apparently, I did not suffer any embolism or decompression sickness mainly because I had not been breathing on compressed air at depth. The assessment was the combination of existing chest or nasal congestion, combined with the rapid descent, had caused the bleeding and loss of air at depth. Recovery took a couple of weeks and was similar to recovering from pneumonia. I could still train naïve animal behaviors back at the base, but I was not able to go to sea for a while.

It was fortunate that Papillion's and Scooner's mine training at sea continued, and eventually we demonstrated the mine shape search and marking in one hundred feet of sea water, indicating that the sea lions could very much be the marine mammal of choice for more advanced mine detection, search, marking, and recovery, if required. There was no word from the navy about whether the sea lions would get the mine recovery mission or not, so there was not any further advanced development of tactics, techniques, procedures, mine targets, or marking equipment for the sea lions. We continued the mine training to maintain the sea lion behaviors, and we continued the basic training of naïve animals.

I had served at Project Quick Find from 1972 to 1977. I managed to get advanced to photographer's mate first class in the process. This was not

Left: My dive buddy John Busch and I display our large catch of sheepshead fish speared on the gunnery range side of San Clemente Island.

Right: I don my wetsuit in preparation for underwater photography of the Quick Find sea lions training at San Clemente Island.

I assist with placing the mock ASROC target in the water from the work barge.

Above: While a trainer with Quick Find, I was able to work with famous underwater photographers, as seen in the far left and far right photos. In the middle photo, I am preparing my own underwater gear for filming at San Clemente Island.

Left: My photojournalism hero Chip Maury, who was instrumental in helping me get accepted to the military photojournalism program and Syracuse University Newhouse School of Communications.

an easy task since I never worked in my rate other than my own personal interest in photography.

Throughout my time at Quick Find, I did get a chance to work with many journalists, photographers, photojournalists, and film production crews. Also timely was that the navy was looking for photographers or journalists to submit portfolios for the military photojournalism program at Syracuse University, Newhouse School of Communications. It would be a one-year program, and it would provide a certificate of completion in military photojournalism, about six credits shy of a bachelor's degree. I knew my marine mammal training time was coming to an end, and I was very excited about applying for this program. As with life, not all things go according to plan. My first portfolio submission was not accepted, but I was fortunate that the navy was still interested in my application, so they provided a former photojournalism graduate to help me with my next portfolio submission. I was also fortunate to have the help of a famous operator and photographer of SEALs, Chip Maury, who was then the photo editor for the *Providence Journal* newspaper.

Professor Fred Demarest, chairman of the Syracuse Photography Department, critiques photographs of military students.

With their help, combined with my Project Quick Find photo story and portfolio, I was accepted into the photojournalism program at Syracuse University. How can one be so blessed to be able to go from one passion to another three times in a row, from SEAL operator, to sea lion trainer, to navy photojournalist? Coincidence, maybe, but more than likely, divine providence.

9
DOG AND PONY SHOWS

The "dog and pony" show was our endearing term for the many sea lion demonstrations we would have to give to visiting dignitaries, whether military, civilian, or politician. We also provided demonstrations for a multitude of print and news media, with occasional requests from film production companies. Add to that the strong interest from friends and families of each of our trainers, and it seemed as if it was a never-ending story.

The easiest dog and pony show was for our friends and families.

This usually meant whoever had the weekend animal watch would take the friends or family members down to the pier and show them how we cleaned the cages, isolated the animals into each of their individual pens with tubs, and gave them vitamins and the feeding regimen. While the working animals were feeding, we would usually break out Gump, the female sea lion, and put her through basic circus-like behaviors, including holding a bucket of fish in her mouth without eating the fish. The most popular was having Gump either kiss the trainer's cheek or salute the trainer. Occasionally, we would let her loose in the water by the pier to show how the animals were free to leave if they wanted, but they always returned for their fish. This releasing demonstration would later prove to be faulty overconfidence.

One time I did have my mom, Patricia Wood, visit Quick Find when we were still located on Pier 13. I took her down to the pens and showed her the same process I mentioned above. The one behavior she became totally enamored with was when Gump would keep giving me a kiss on the

Above: The original Quick Find team members gather with their sea lions on the work barge for Bill Barrada, who was doing a story about the program for *Skin Diver* magazine.

Right: I demonstrate the hand salute with my favorite sea lion, Sinbad, during one of many exhibitions for family and friends.

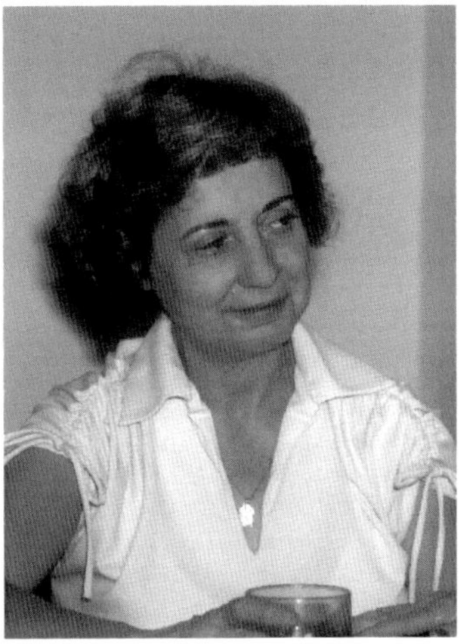

My mom, Patricia Wood.

cheek. My mom was absolutely convinced that Gump "loved" me. I tried to explain to her that this was anthropomorphism, or attribution of human characteristics to an animal. "No, no, no, she loves you, I can tell!" I had to tell her to just watch how much the animals loved me after they had eaten, had a full belly, and were released out of their pens and back into the pool for socializing. I took Gump back to the pens and fed her. She was the last to eat, so when she was finished, I released all the animals from their individual pens into the common deck and pool area. I attempted to get Gump's attention and have her kiss me or salute me. I did not try this with Fatman. Sure enough, I can only imagine that Gump thought I had been smoking dope or something. She wasn't about to perform without a fish reward. She must have thought I was nuts. Now I was the one anthropomorphizing. Stated a little more accurately, Gump totally ignored me and would not give me the time of day. She went back into the pool.

Another family and friend demonstration involved bringing Sinbad out of the pen and onto the work barge where we had a dressing stand. I wanted to show my friends and family how this former naïve volunteer animal was progressing into a working animal. I harnessed Sinbad on the dressing stand and had him hold a grabber device. I hooked up a reel of line and let Sinbad jump off the barge into the water and come back to the stand for a fish reward, which he did without my having to pull on the tether line. Here's where my confidence in Sinbad got me in trouble. I decided to remove the line from Sinbad's harness and let him go into the water near the piers. I had another trainer there helping me with this demonstration. Much to my disappointment, Sinbad would not return to the barge, much less the dressing stand. I felt my face well up with embarrassment. I kept slapping on the dressing stand and showing Sinbad his fish reward. About thirty minutes later, when Sinbad still would not return to the barge, I decided to lure him with fish into the community pool. This involved putting all the other animals back into their individual pens, which they did not appreciate. Then I had to deal with difficult-to-remove staples from the top of the pool netting to drop one corner of the net into the water so I could lure Sinbad into the

Sometimes it seemed we should change the name to Project Quick Find Demonstration Team. On the left, I have Sinbad give me a kiss on the cheek for an audience of family and friends. On the right, I show a group of VIPs how Sinbad would mount the dressing stand and hold the D8 grabber device on his nose.

pool. Eureka! That idea worked, and Sinbad swam into the pool for a fish reward while still wearing his harness.

My associate quickly pulled up and reattached the top of the pool net, and now Sinbad was at least back in the pen. It had been quite a long time, so I told all the visitors it would be best that they leave. I could not leave Sinbad in the pool wearing his harness. We were always concerned that some part of the harness would catch on the bottom of the net and the sea lion could not surface and would drown. I had to get him out of the pool. I still had some confidence in Sinbad's responsiveness to commands. Again, I slapped the dressing stand in the pen signaling Sinbad to come out of the water and mount the stand. I tried that several times with no response from the now very stubborn Sinbad. I even put fish near the deck edge of the pool entrance, to no avail. I had two options left, one of which I really did not want to use, and that was a hoop net to lift him out of the water. The second idea was to have my associate lure Sinbad with fish in the water to the pool entrance. I would climb along the pool's inside deck walkway and,

Left: The floating pen at San Clemente Island, with the animals swimming in the community pool.

Right: Tom McHugh prepares a harness at the floating pen in Coronado to let the animals out of the community pool.

with one hand for support and leverage on the fence, would lean over and grab the top strap of Sinbad's harness and pull him out of the water. This, I thought, was the better of the two plans. Well, it worked exactly as I had planned. Sinbad was distracted by the fish reward, and I was able to grab his harness and pull him up and out of the water. He was not that heavy, so it was easy enough to do. Here is where the plan deviated due to some things I hadn't thought of, such as how was I going to edge my way along the inside of the pool back to the fence opening when I had a sea lion in one hand and my other hand providing support and gripping on the fence. The other thing I did not think of was how Sinbad was going to react to this entirely new behavioral event. I'll tell you how: he reacted just like any wild animal would react when surprised and threatened. As I was gripping one hand on the fence and one holding Sinbad, he decided to make a meal out of my wrist and forearm and began to bite the crap out of my skinny arm with his canines. I could not let Sinbad go, so I let him keep biting my arm, with blood now spurting out. I yelled to my fellow trainer to grab Sinbad from me and put him on the deck. "No way!" he yelled and left the pen area, leaving me alone with this wild animal munching on my arm. The only option I had left was to swing Sinbad back and forth in the air and try to throw him through the gate opening onto the pen deck, hoping I could get out of the cage quick enough to close the gate before he slipped back into the water. Luckily for me, that plan did work. I threw Sinbad onto the pen deck, climbed out of the inside pool fence decking, and closed the cage door in time. Now Sinbad was huffing and puffing while waddling around the deck barking. I let him settle down and once again patted the dressing stand, and Sinbad jumped right up onto the stand and let me unharness him without any further problems. I opened the pool gate, let all the other sea lions out of their pens, and all was back to normal in the sea lion world. It was not until I left the pen and locked the pen door that I started to feel the shock and adrenalin of the situation. I did take that time to yell at my trainer associate for being a wimp and abandoning me in the cage. I never forgave or trusted him again. Yes, the situation was my fault, but he could have helped. Definitely a learning experience for me, especially after going through the thirteen stitches they had to put in my arm at the base dispensary. The stitches weren't bad; it was the cleaning of the wound with antiseptic and the tetanus shot pain that forever placed this incident into my memory banks.

Other easier demonstrations usually occurred on QAST shots when TV and print media folks would show up to write and film about this unique sea lion missile recovery program. Gordy Sybrant usually handled these media events on a QAST shot, but if one of our officers was traveling with us, they

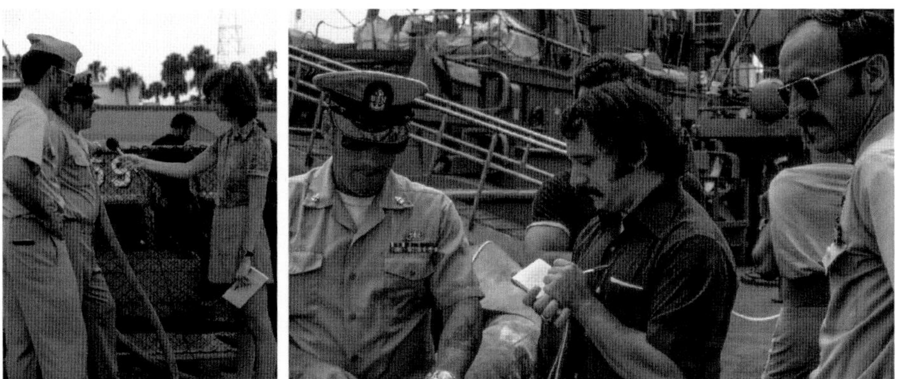

Chief Gordy Sybrant and LT Paul Plumb speak with reporters during a VIP day on the navy support ship in Norfolk, Virginia, prior to an ASROC mission.

Trainer Bud Dennehy and Akahi look eye-to-eye at the end of the long working day before removing the harness and letting Akahi join the other animals in the community pool.

were sure to be involved in the media presentation. Gordy just wanted to do it to make sure the media folks were getting accurate information and not exaggerating any of their stories. The officer was usually involved for the media exposure. These QAST shot demonstrations generally never involved any circus-like performance from the animals for a couple of good reasons. One was we did not want the media to think these were circus animals.

Secondly, QAST shots involved our largest and most dominant sea lions like Fatman and Akahi, and neither of these animals was too tolerant of performing circus acts. Another reason was that too much confusing activity, with multiple people present, big film equipment, extra noise, and generally a lot of unfamiliar activity, would sometimes make the animals nervous. One time during a media event, Tom McHugh brought Fatman on the dressing stand simply to put on his harness, a behavior he had performed hundreds of times. There was some extra activity and confusion going on from the media, and when Tom turned his head and gazed away, Fatman grabbed the biceps on his arm and shook it around like it was a rag doll. Tom got Fatman to release his arm, and he immediately undressed Fatman and put him back into the portable pen on the ship. Keep in mind, the animals are

Chief Gordy Sybrant and LT Paul Plumb speak with reporters during VIP day in Norfolk.

already wary about being in a new location and on a ship or boat that has a lot of extra ambient noise. Exposing these dominant animals to additional confusion can be hazardous. Tom had to get several stitches in his arm, but he stayed with us and performed on the QAST shot.

Some of the most burdensome sea lion demonstrations usually occurred with visiting military, government service, or political dignitaries. These were especially burdensome because the demonstration timing was totally controlled by the schedule of the dignitaries, regardless of whether the animals already had a long day and were already fed or not. It also meant that we were attired in our best and most starched green uniforms and hats trying to handle wet and poopy sea lions and trying to keep them calm while we waited for the dignitary to finally show up late. These demonstrations would occur regardless of time, day or night. Luckily for us, the dignitaries' schedules were usually very condensed, which meant we would have a short and sweet demonstration of just putting a sea lion on the dressing stand and letting the dignitary touch the animal if desired. Of course that came with a warning from the trainer to the dignitary to proceed at his own risk. Usually, we had Gump on the stand so there really was no real risk involved, but it was good to watch the dignitary react a little. Maybe there was a little childish "payback" involved by the trainer because of the inconvenience of the situation. I will never confirm or deny the truth of this.

Of all the types of demonstrations we conducted, the film production events were the ones that were the most work but were also the most fun. These events were fairly convenient because the film crews usually adapted to our schedules and accompanied us during normal training days at sea. Occasionally, it would mean working on the weekends, but that was not too often. The film production events that were the most memorable were Mutual of

Top: Star of the Omaha Mutual *Wild Kingdom* series, Marlin Perkins gets a kiss on the cheek from Akahi during the filming of the show.

Bottom: Perkins feeds Akahi a reward fish as trainer Rick Hetzell supervises the demonstration.

Omaha's *Wild Kingdom* with Marlin Perkins and *The Mike Douglas Talk Show*. One event that helped me the most was a *Skin Diver* magazine feature story.

Mutual of Omaha's *Wild Kingdom* TV show involved its main actor, Marlin Perkins, scuba diving on our ASROC training targets, as well as riding in the Z-bird with the sea lions during training at sea. He had very recognizable silver hair that needed to be visible during all filming, and that meant he could not wear a wetsuit hood while diving underwater. The water temperatures in the ocean off Point Loma were in the low sixty degrees. He also had to wear his wetsuit topside all day long in the sun so he could be ready at any moment to get in the water with his underwater film crew. He was one of the toughest older guys I had ever seen, and despite the fact that he was the TV show star, he never grumbled or complained.

The director of *Wild Kingdom* was not pleased with the underwater visibility off Point Loma, so he asked Gordy if there was anywhere they could film the underwater scenes. Gordy suggested they could film off Santa Catalina Island, just "twenty-six miles across the sea," as the song says. That, of course, was a significant logistic and expensive issue. My understanding is the show paid the costs, but we used a Navy LCU and loaded everyone, animals, and equipment onboard and used the LCU as our base of operations off the coast of Santa Catalina.

A high view of the casino and Avalon Harbor at Santa Catalina Island, where the final scenes of the *Wild Kingdom* episodes covering Project Quick Find were filmed.

Above: Project Quick Find was featured on the daily *Mike Douglas Show*.

Left: Underwater photograph of a sea lion properly placing the D9 grabber device on the mock-ASROC target tail cone.

The LCU anchored offshore of Catalina to take advantage of the much clearer waters. Now the *Wild Kingdom* underwater film crew could set up its equipment and film the sea lion locating and attaching the grabber device on the mock-ASROC target.

The Mike Douglas Show was a daytime television talk show that ran from 1961 to 1982. This particular production did require weekend work and adapting to the show schedule, but the good news was it was filmed at the Coronado Boy Scout boat ramp only five hundred yards from our Quick Find building and sea lion pens. This was also a Fourth of July weekend that included a full-scale Naval Special Warfare demonstration of Underwater Demolition Team (UDT) and Sea, Air, Land (SEAL) operational demonstrations, so we were not the only ones working on a holiday. Mike Douglas interviewed the movie actor Cliff Robertson, who also rode in an SDV to the boat ramp pier and hopped on the pier for a closeup demonstration by trainer Mike Kelley and Akahi on the dressing stand. Mike Douglas attempted to interview Akahi, but since he would not participate, Mike interviewed our OIC at that time, LT Don Ridgeway, along with the trainer Mike Kelley. The inshore undersea warfare group commander was present and participated in the interview. Cliff Robertson did manage to elicit a cheek kiss from Akahi for a fish reward. A sea lion was on standby in a Z-bird nearby just in case Akahi did not like all of the noise and activity, but he not only behaved but also put up with a little of the circus performance. Akahi stole the show.

Trainer Mike Kelley watches closely as sea lion Akahi kisses the movie star Cliff Robertson. TV star Mike Douglas and Quick Find OIC LT Don Ridgeway watch the scene.

Mike Douglas interviewed the movie actor Cliff Robertson.

Left: Akahi places the D5 training grabber in the proper location on the mock-ASROC training target for a photo that ended up as the cover and poster for *Skin Diver* magazine.

Right: Chief Gordon Sybrant, me, and John Busch show our sea lions to *Skin Diver* magazine writer Bill Barrada.

The *Skin Diver* magazine event was pretty simple and nonintrusive. The writer, Bill Barrada, simply accompanied us out to sea for standard ASROC recovery training off Point Loma. What made this memorable was that the writer and *Skin Diver* asked me to do the underwater photography for this article, and I gladly obliged. Those were still film days, so I used my Nikonos-III underwater camera with dual strobes and a 15mm wide-angle lens borrowed from Combat Camera Group. Underwater visibility off Point Loma varied quite often due to sea and weather conditions, so I used the widest-angle lens available so I could get as close to the ASROC mock-up target as possible to catch the sea lion placing one of the grabber devices on the tail cone of the target. We knew that we would need to go deep enough for clearer water and for the sea lion but shallow enough for the diver. We settled on putting the target at ninety feet to maximize diver bottom time but also keep the target deep enough for the animal. Luckily on this day, the sea conditions were flat, and the water visibility at ninety feet deep was a good thirty feet, making it ideal conditions for underwater photography. The only drawback was that at the ninety-foot depth, it got dark, which reduced the chances for seeing the sea lion approach the target. The photographer had to be ready to shoot with no notice because the sea lion's approach blended into the dark background. Seeing the sea lion hitting the target with the grabber would almost be a surprise every time. This photography assignment literally lived up to the saying "capturing the moment."

We only had a moment to photograph from when the sea lion hit the target and disappeared, ascending to the surface. Magazines required color slides in those days, so I had to wait several days for the slides to get processed and mounted before I knew whether I got any useable images. There were a couple of nervous days having to wait. I did not want to mess up my first opportunity for shooting for a popular magazine. There was no pay with this assignment, but there were credit lines that could help get me established as a photographer. The results were great! I got several usable images to be included in the article, with one of them turning into a poster for *Skin Diver* magazine, as well as the cover photograph. That photograph is also the cover photo for this book; it shows a sea lion diving and implanting a D5 grabber onto the training ASROC target.

10

PHOTOJOURNALISM AND PROJECT QUICK FIND

Photographing for *Skin Diver* magazine ended up being a great opportunity for my soon-to-be new life in military photojournalism. In 1977, my wife and I loaded up my blue Dodge van with all of our household goods and drove across country from San Diego to Syracuse, New York. That was our first experience of living in snow, which totalled over 180 inches that year. I attended the Newhouse School of Communications at Syracuse University for a year. That was one of the most challenging years of my life, but that story is for another book. Once I graduated from Syracuse, I had to temporarily leave the SEAL community and serve as a regular navy photographer assigned on a tour as a military photojournalist. That change of duty station led me to the Chief of Naval Technical Training Command (CNTECHTRA) in Millington, Tennessee, as the staff photojournalist. This command had all the navy's technical training schools under its command, which included Basic Underwater Demolition SEAL (BUD/S) training in Coronado, California. I decided to do a photo story about BUD/S training, and while I was there in Coronado, I decided to do a story on Project Quick Find to see how the program had progressed since I had left two years prior. Project Quick Find was not technically under CNTECHTRA command, but the staff public affairs officer for whom I worked did not mind me staying extra time in Coronado to do the story on Project Quick Find. It was still a sought-after and interesting story to be told, and I had arranged for the story to be published in the navy's *Faceplate* magazine.

Project QUICK FIND

a "special" unit in spec warfare

Navy Faceplate Magazine

My story on Project Quick Find appeared in the navy's *Faceplate* magazine.

My good friend and fellow BUD/S class-55 mate Marshall Dean Daugherty was the LT and OIC of Project Quick Find. This was fortuitous because it helped me gain full access to photographing and writing about the project. I knew some things would have changed at Quick Find in the last two years. I was pleased to see the progress that they had made. There were still a few trainers at Quick Find whom I knew, such as Bud Dennehy, who was now the lead trainer. Dennehy had become Fatman's trainer. It was interesting that in two years, Project Quick Find had begun training sea lions for both the mine mission and continuing the ASROC recovery mission.

The latter ASROC mission was occurring in deeper depths, with potential for a recovery as deep as 750 feet. LT Daugherty, the current Quick Find OIC, had come up with an innovative solution to train the sea lions to this deeper depth. Training sea lions off Point Loma for the maximum depth of 500 feet required daily transits to almost five miles off Point Loma. This resulted in a total thirty-four-mile round-trip transit every day, which added a lot of extra transit time, made training days much longer and fuel costs much higher. Trying to find the new 750-foot maximum water depth off Point Loma would add many more miles and hours to the already burdensome time and distance. It was LT Daugherty's idea to temporarily move the sea lions to San Clemente Island (SCI), where 750 feet of water depth was just a couple miles offshore. It was a secure military land and water area, and the water was pristine compared to Point Loma. LT Daugherty took his trainer personnel, sea lions, pens, boats, and all required equipment to SCI for about four months. They trained during the week, and the trainers would fly home for the weekend, except for the watch stander, who had watch and stayed the weekend.

Personnel who worked on SCI were LT Dean Daugherty, Bud Dennehy, Bill Check, and one trainer who passed away during that time, Harry Bush. The sea lions were Gigi and Andy. Gigi was the sea lion that was able to dive to the 750-foot depth.

Right: My good friend and OIC of Project Quick Find, LT Marshall Dean Daugherty carries a sea lion down the long gangway to the floating pier and dock at San Clemente Island. Being carried was a new behavior the sea lions needed to learn.

Below: Akahi jumps back into the rubber boat, splashing trainer Bud Dennehy while training at sea out on San Clemente Island.

Project Quick Find crew at San Clemente Island. *Left to right*: LT Dean Daugherty, Harry Busch, Bill Check, and Bud Dennehy, holding Gigi the sea lion that dove 750 feet to recover an ASROC.

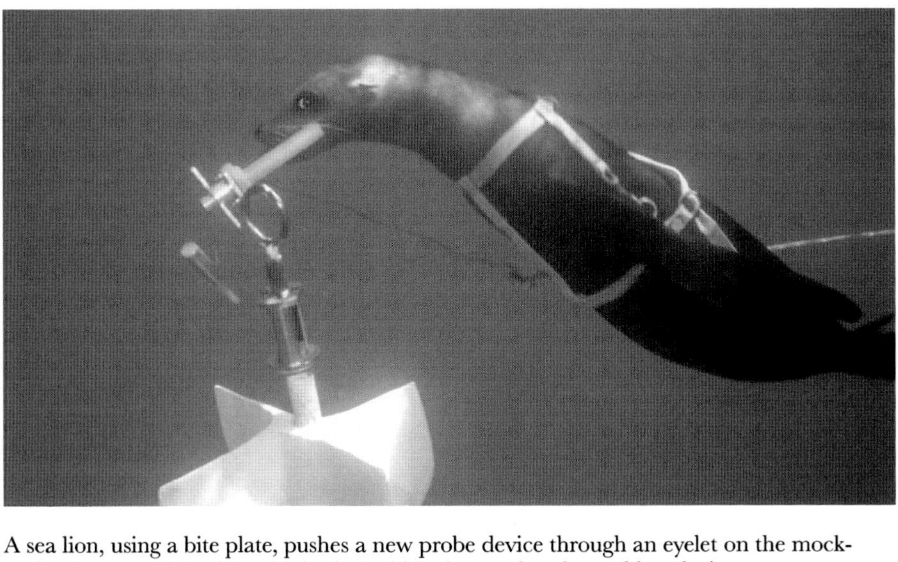

A sea lion, using a bite plate, pushes a new probe device through an eyelet on the mock-ASROC trainer. Working with both the bite plate and probe grabber devices were new behaviors the animals needed to learn.

Top: Sea lion sits on Bud Dennehy's lap with LT Dean Daugherty in the passenger seat as they drive to the pier at San Clemente Island. Learning to ride in the truck front seat was a new behavior for the sea lions, which they learned quickly.

Bottom: Bud Dennehy carries his sea lion up the steep and long gangway at San Clemente Island pier.

The move to SCI also helped with the new mine mission, where the trainers could place the mock mine target in shallower water with forty- to fifty-foot water visibility, enabling the trainer to watch whether the sea lion contacted the right section of the mine. Normally, this would require placing a scuba diver in the water to signal with a buoy on the surface that the sea lion hit the right target. SCI clear water eliminated that scuba diver observation requirement. The move to SCI did add to some additional behaviors for the animals to learn. In some cases, the new behaviors were simply logistical in that the sea lion needed to learn to ride in the pickup truck and learn to walk or be carried down a very long and steep gangway to get from the SCI pier down to the floating boat dock that was a good twenty feet below.

The other new behaviors were operational. The mine project changed from a grabber mechanism on a bite plate or nose cone to a probe device on a bite plate. The sea lions needed to learn how to place the probe device through a padeye on the tail of an ASROC target or on the mine target. This probe-to-padeye behavior was a little more difficult for the sea lions to master, but it was a significant improvement over the much more cumbersome mine grabber device, which was significantly larger in size than the new probe

Sea lion just misses placing the new probe grabber device through the eyelet on the tail of the mock-ASROC trainer. This probe grabber/eyelet system was later used for both ASROC and mine recoveries.

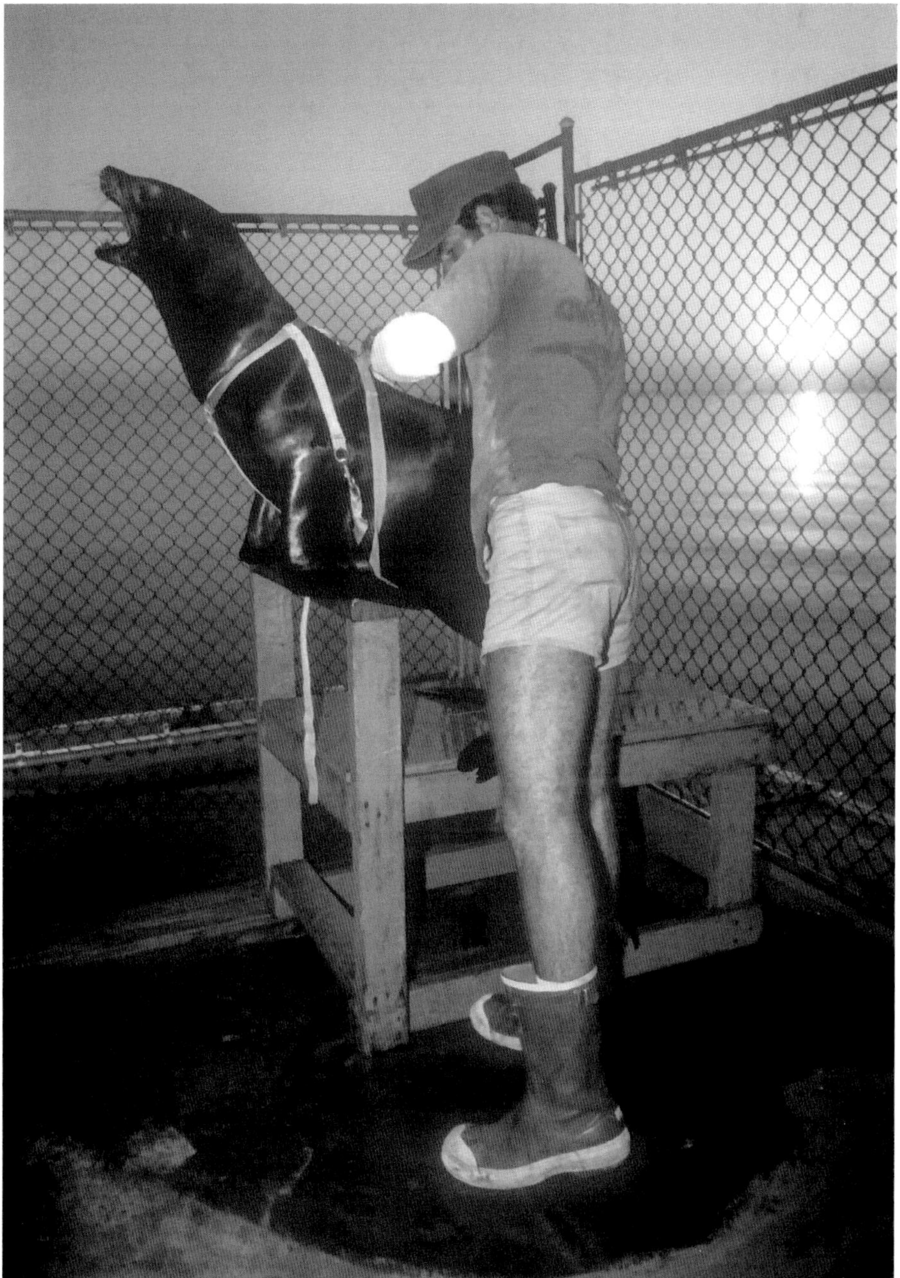

Grumpy Fatman is impatient for his reward of fish as Bud Dennehy removes his harness at the end of a long training day. Fatman could care less about the beautiful sunset behind him. He just wants his fish!

As a navy photojournalist covering Project Quick Find, I was published in *National Geographic World*, *Skin Diver* magazine, *Reader's Digest*, and multiple other civilian and military magazines and papers across the country.

device. This QF group did one mine recovery demonstration in Charleston, South Carolina, after an ASROC recovery. CAPT Christianson from MINERON 12 asked if the mine recovery could be done, and LT Daugherty said they could do it in two weeks. The previous work of changing the sea lions from the nose cone to the bite-plate mechanism enabled the sea lions to make multiple attempts to place the probe grabber into the mine padeye. The bite-plate probe-grabber system also enabled the sea lions to improve the ASROC recovery to one connection every time. Under LT Daugherty's leadership, this group of trainers had advanced the Project Quick Find capabilities significantly in both the ASROC and mine missions.

This completed my association with Project Quick Find in 1978; I look back and realize what a tremendous opportunity and blessing I had of transitioning through three distinct and separate occupations as a SEAL point man, sea lion trainer, and navy photojournalist. Project Quick Find sea lion recovery of objects from the sea floor still continues to this day but under different program names.

The program and names of the trainers and sea lions have all changed, but the spirit of Project Quick Find continues.

ABOUT THE AUTHOR

Author CDR Michael P. Wood (USN Ret.) tells the story of Project Quick Find. He served as a Navy SEAL point man in Vietnam but transferred to Project Quick Find, where he used his navy photographer and marine mammal trainer experience to document the program from 1972 to 1979.

Left to right: Author as Navy SEAL point man, navy-trained photographer, and sea lion trainer.